I0483287

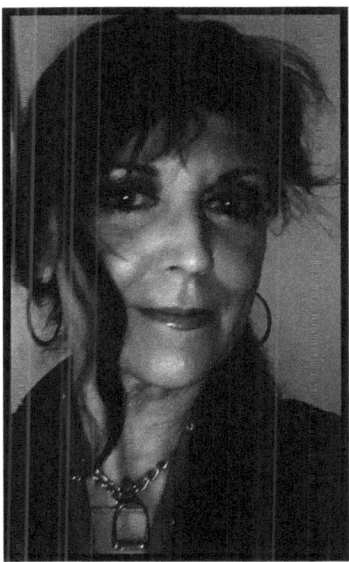

Kay Eastwood is the author and artist of *Love and Light*. Her paintings accompany a lifetime of wisdom, primarily passed down by family elders. These images push the boundaries of the written word. This book is inspiring and fascinating, embodying the idea that 'a picture may be worth a thousand words.'

The yoga images were inspired by an art commission to the Canary Islands and by yoga instruction from Elder David Sye, promoting a healthy body, mind, and soul.

This unique combination of words and images is eloquent and open to interpretation by the reader. Kay has ensured that this thought-provoking work will linger with the reader long after they have turned the last page.

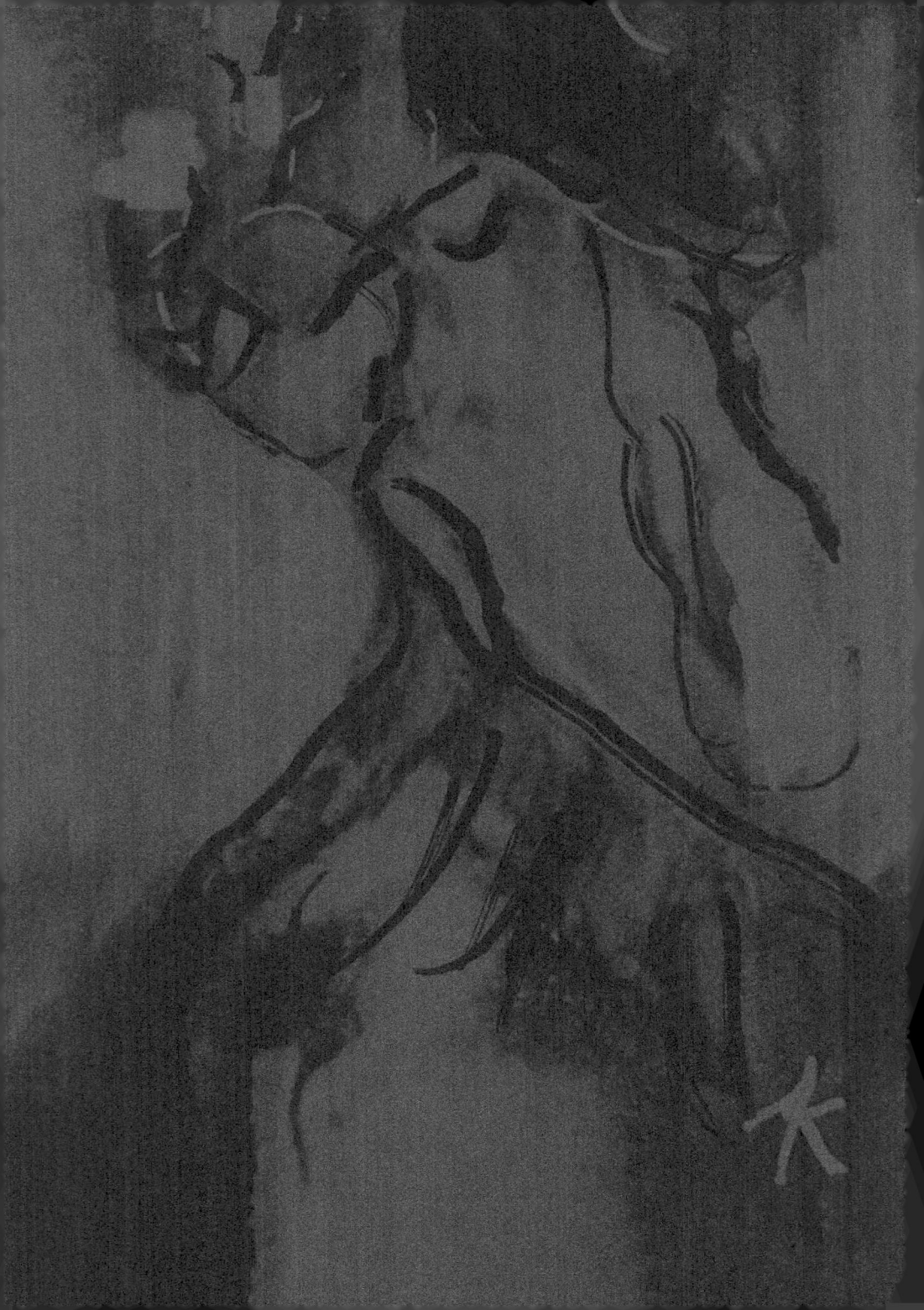

Love and Light

Kay Eastwood

AUSTIN MACAULEY PUBLISHERS™

LONDON • CAMBRIDGE • NEW YORK • SHARJAH

A CIP catalogue record for this title is available from the British Library.

ISBN 9781528976442 (Paperback)
ISBN 9781528976459 (ePub e-book)

www.austinmacauley.com

First Published 2024
Austin Macauley Publishers Ltd®
1 Canada Square
Canary Wharf
London
E14 5AA

Thank you to my daughter Ursula and my son, Rory.

My first readers, first everything.

And to all my family and friends.

To Sarah and our three baby buddhas Daniel, Emily and Gabriel, who make everything daily bring joy.

Paul, Brendan, Denis and Desmond, for being a constant presence of love and light in my life.

To Arts Council Ireland and Visual Arts Ireland for the opportunity to work in artists' studios.

Tyrone Guthrie, Art Centre Ireland, Vallauris S. France, and Arts, Letters, Numbers Residency Albany New York.

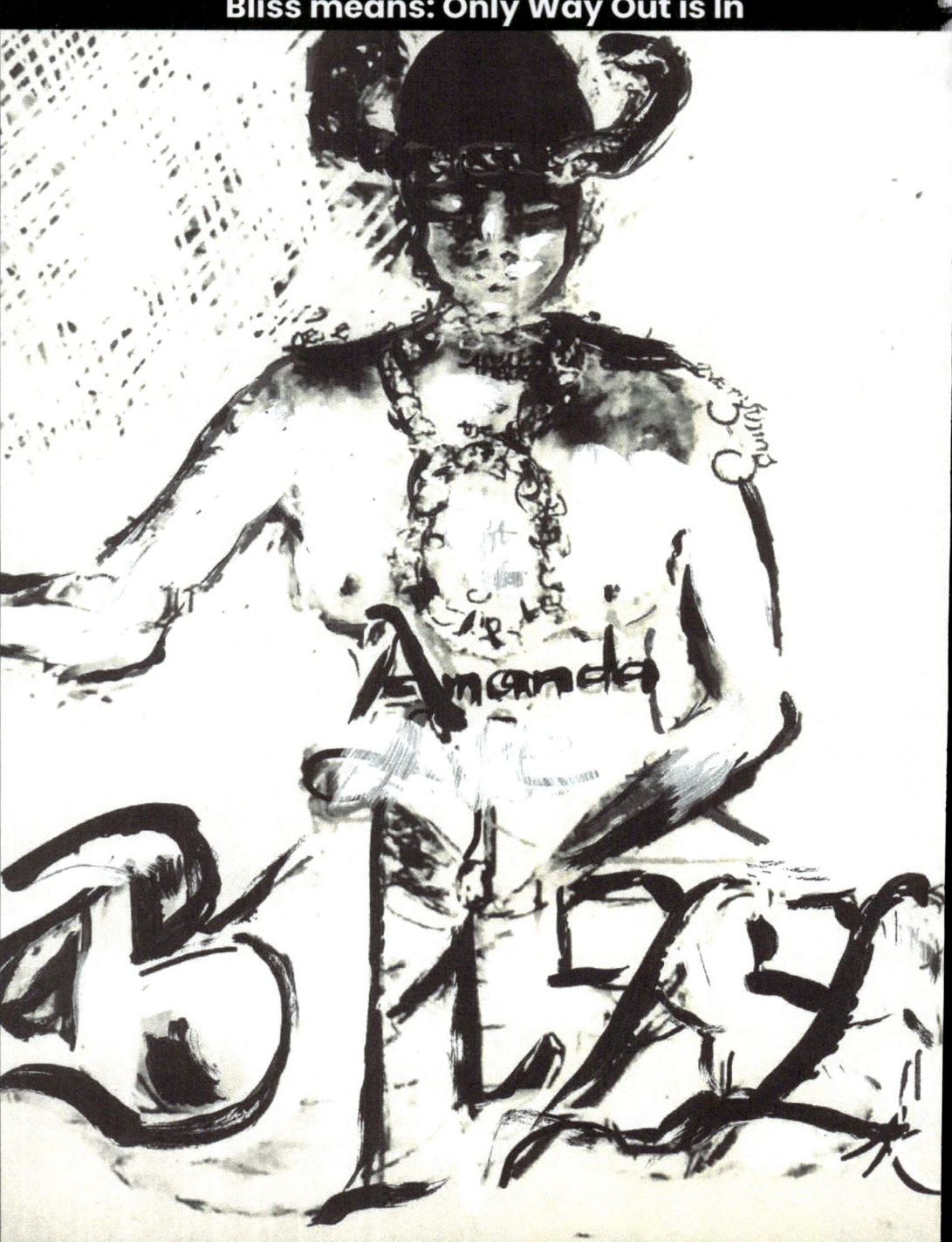

The Wise Master Themselves

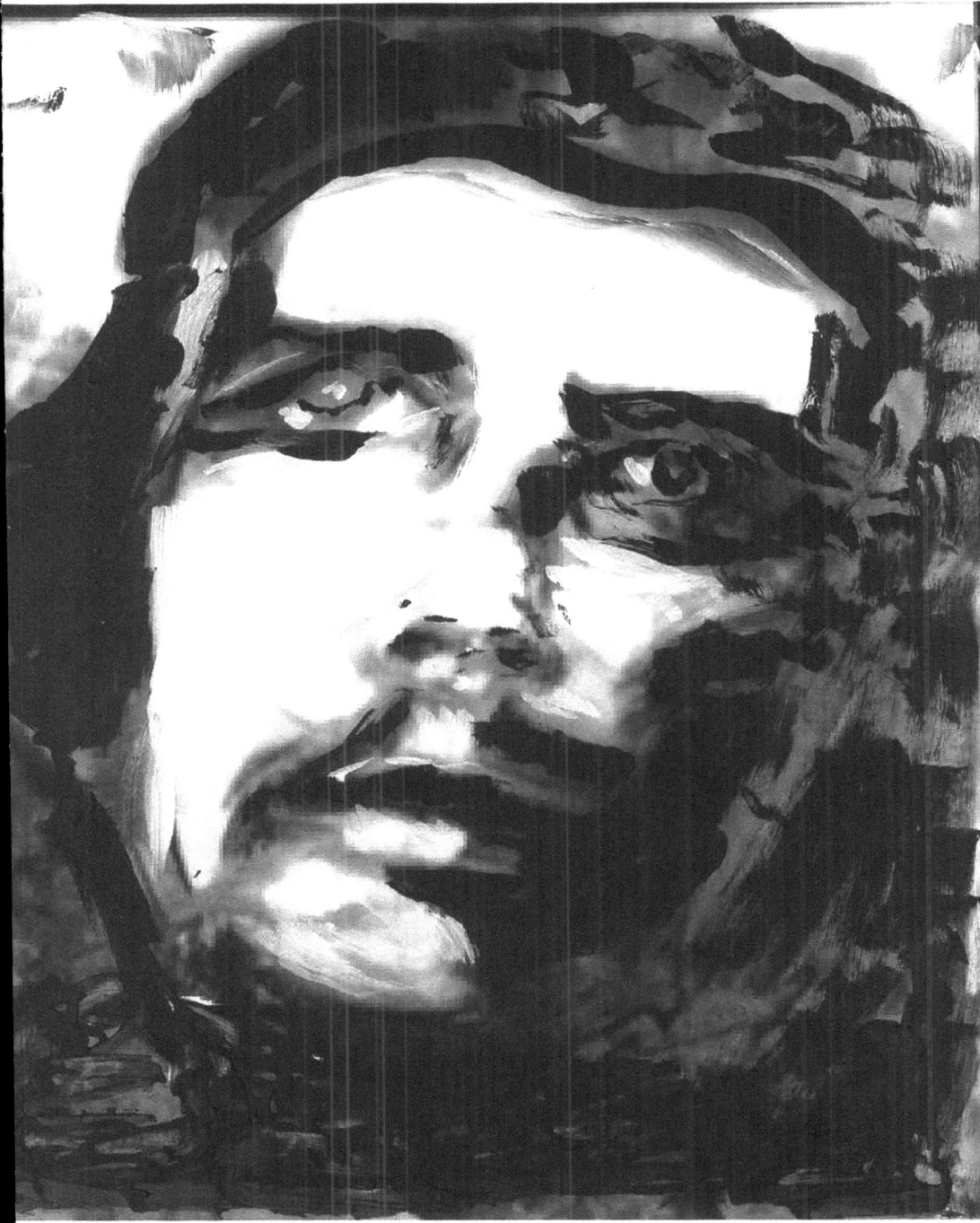

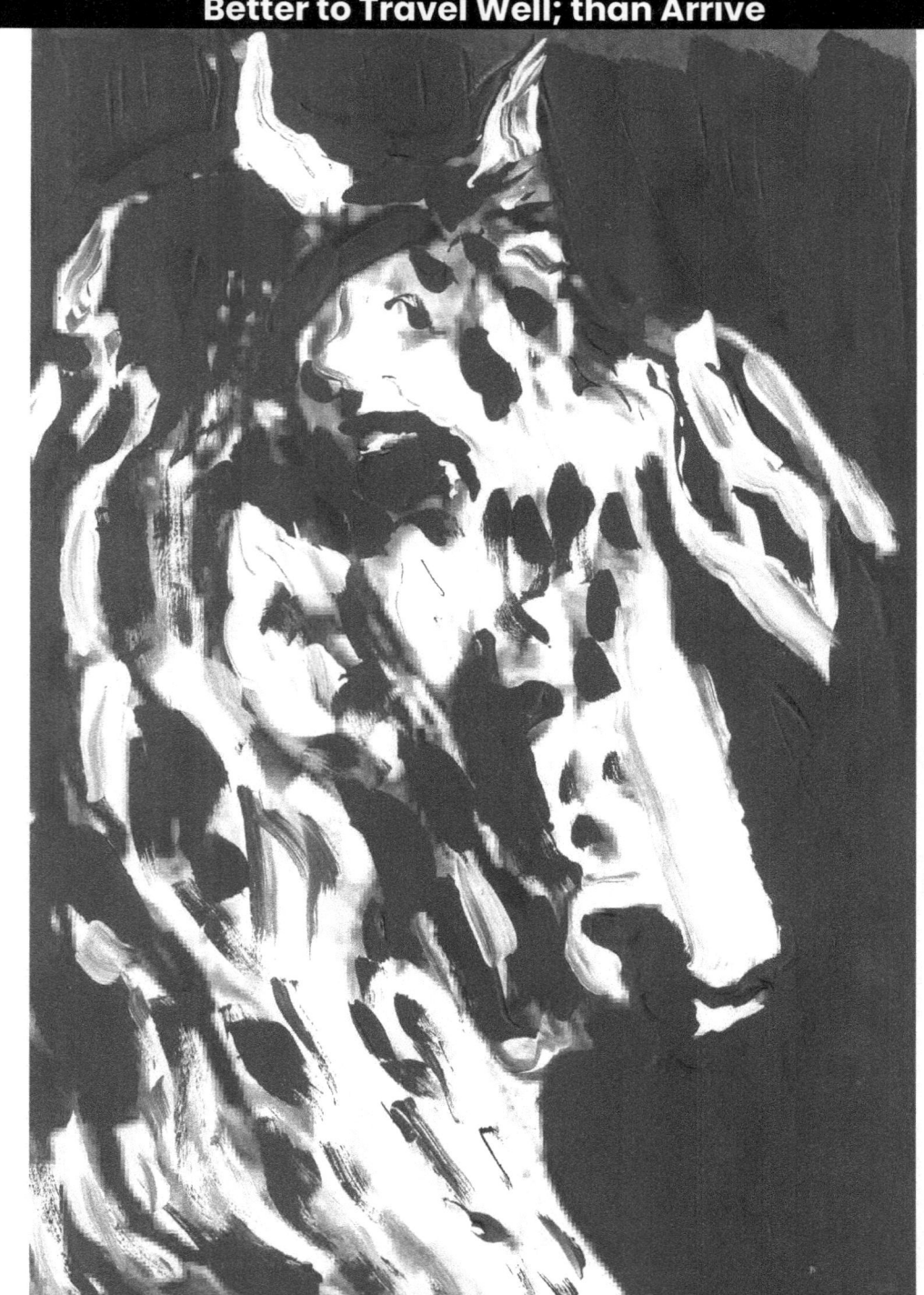

The Root of All Suffering is Attachment

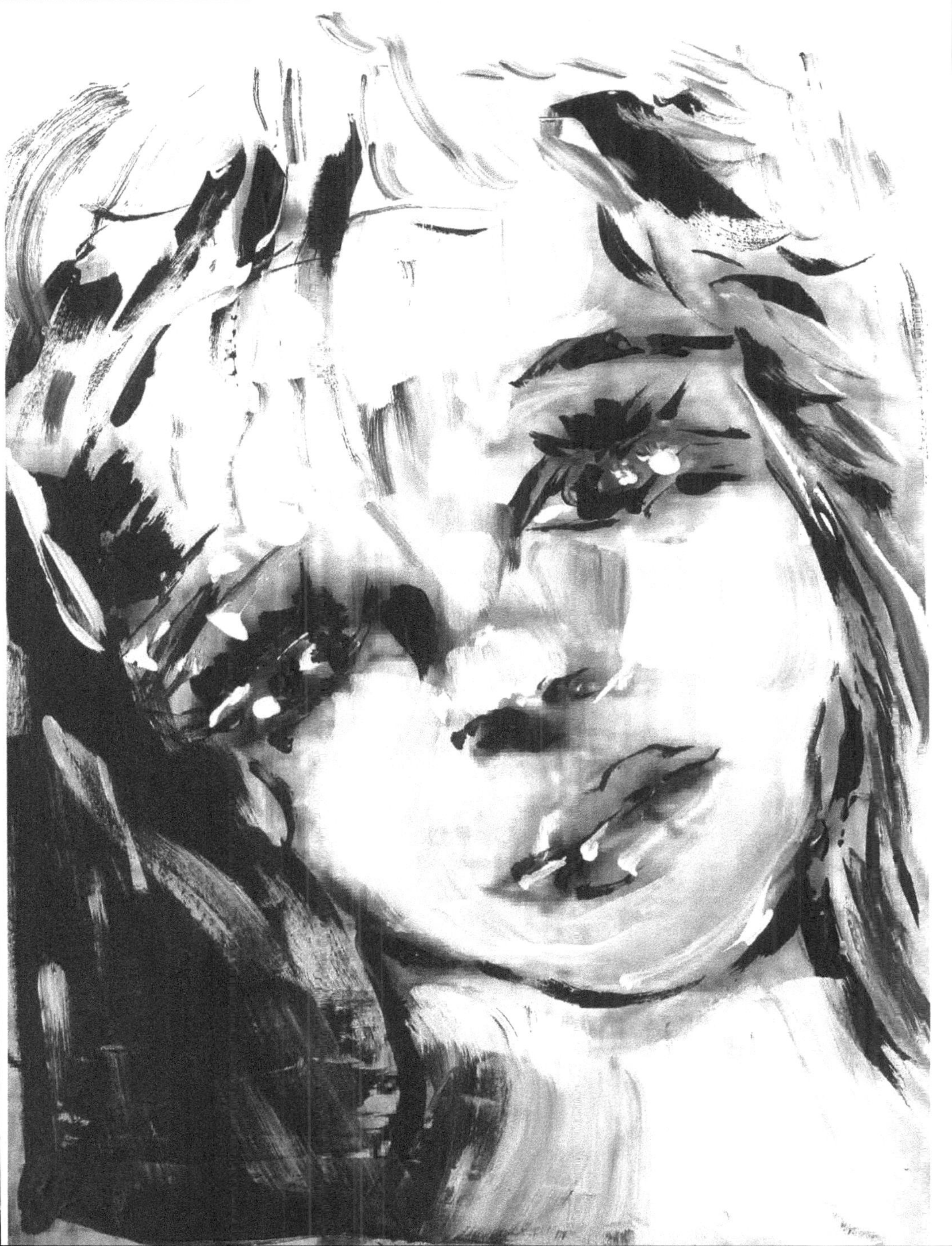

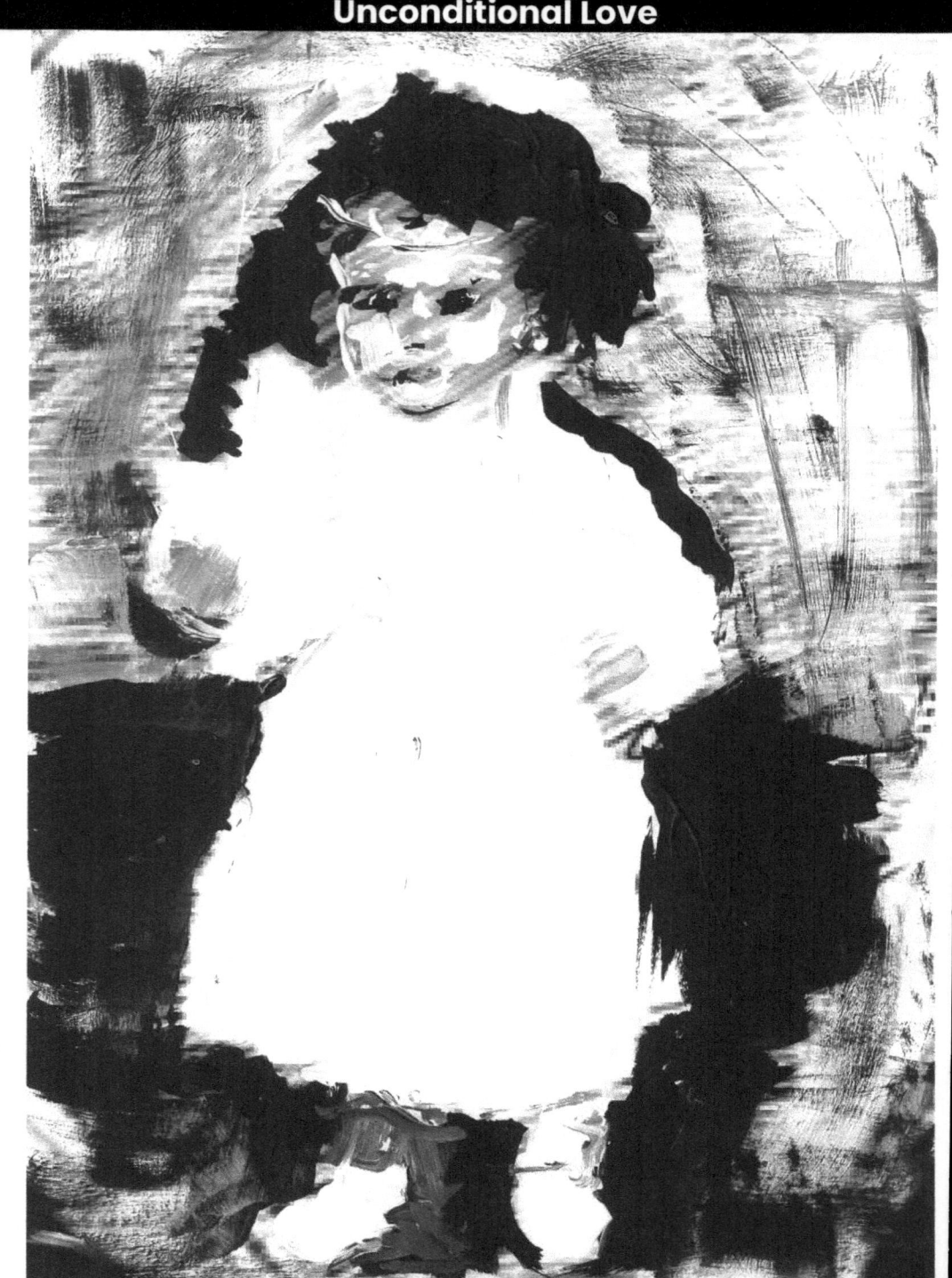

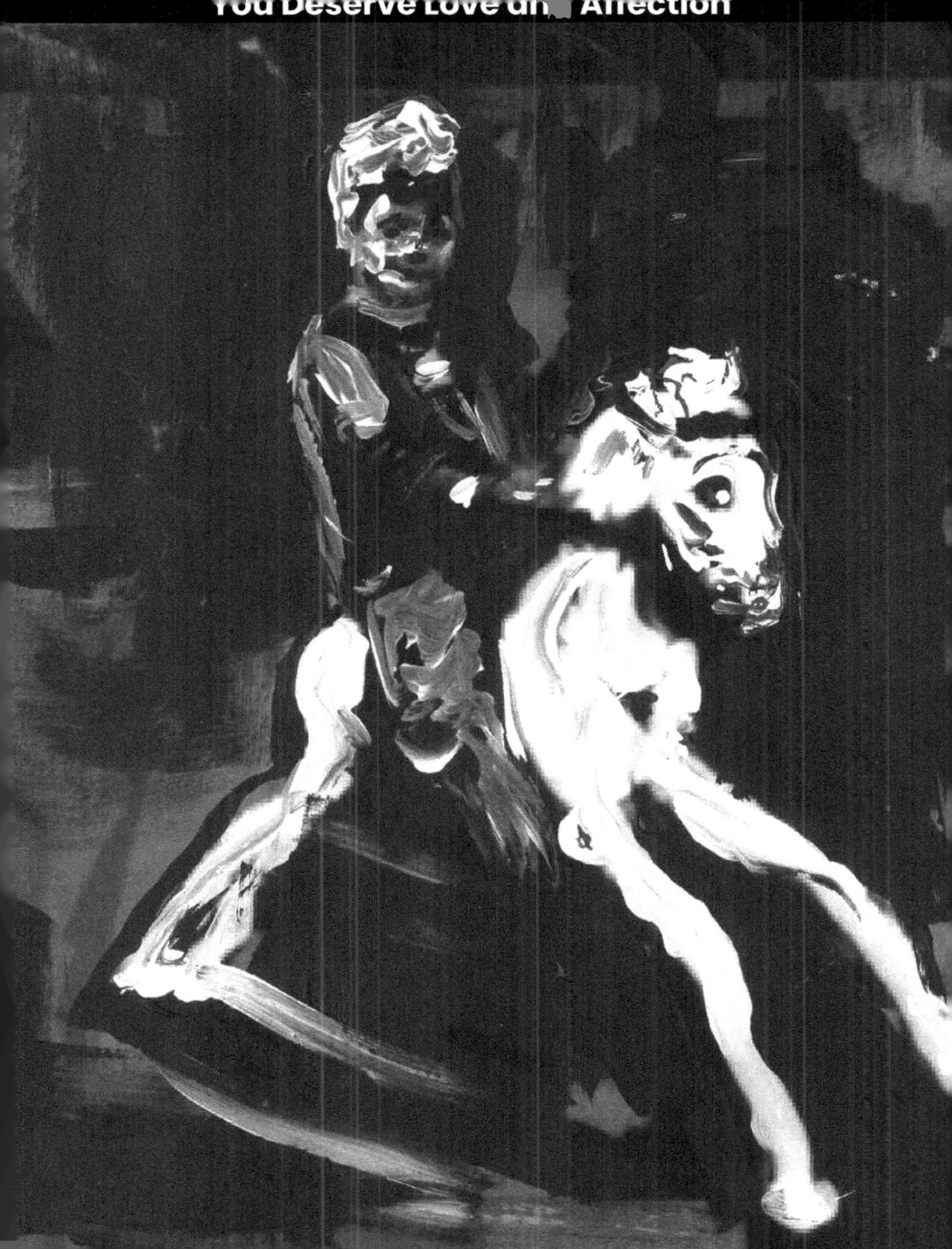

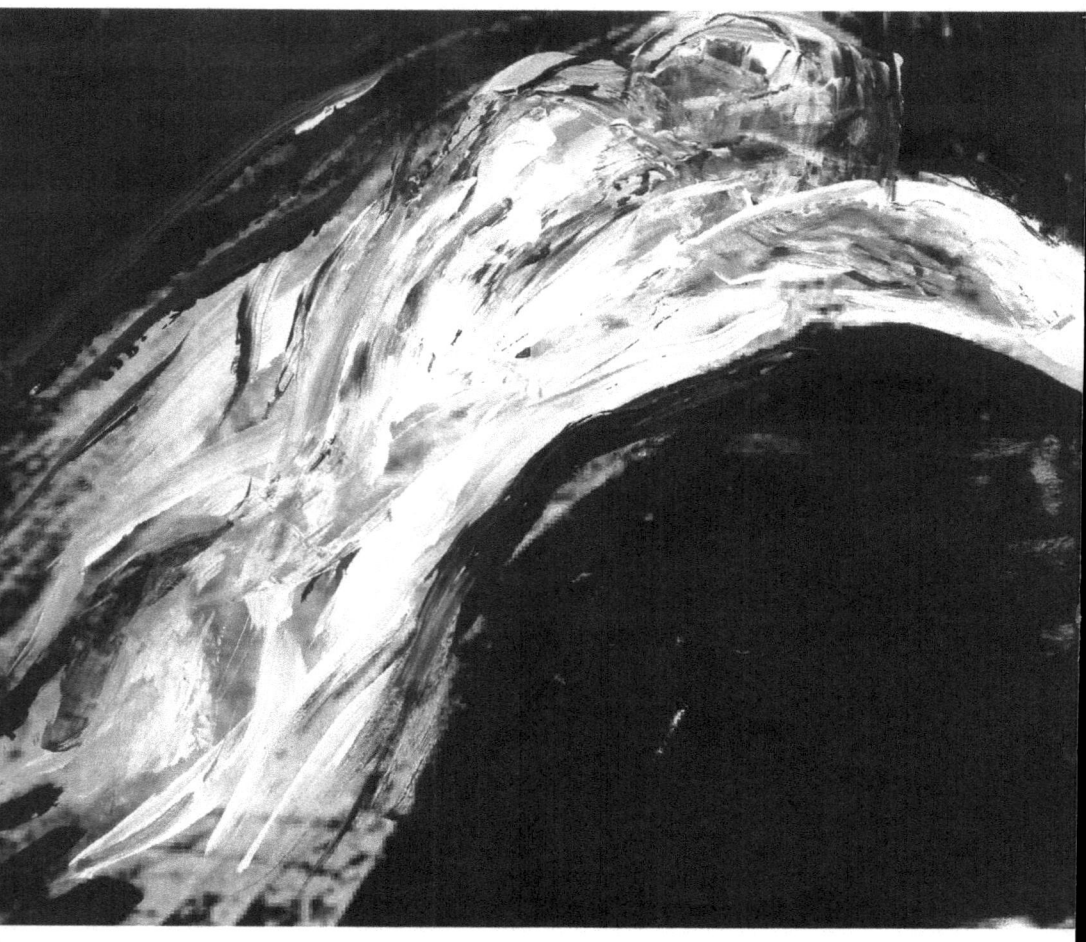

Change is Never Painful, Resistance to Change Hurts

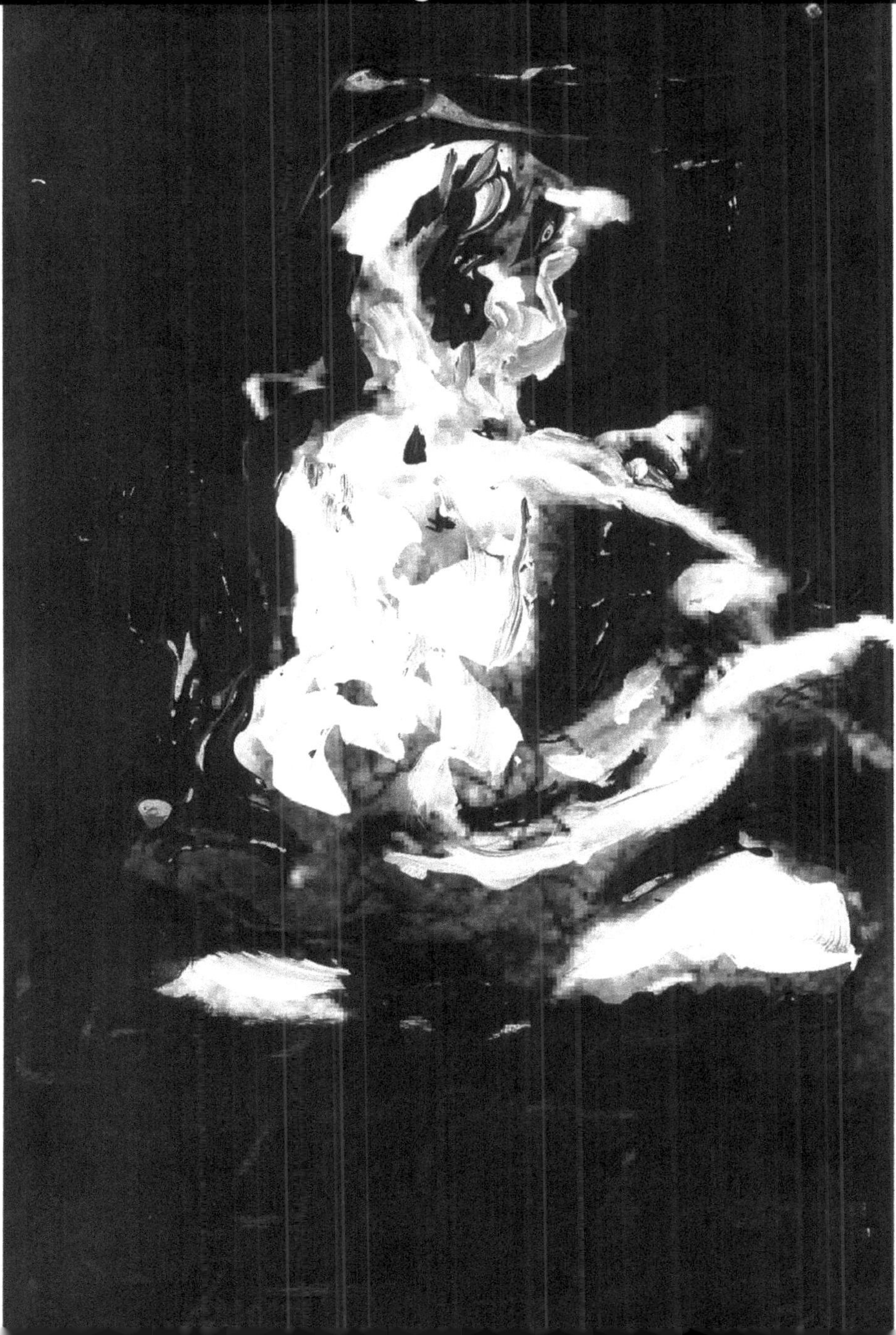

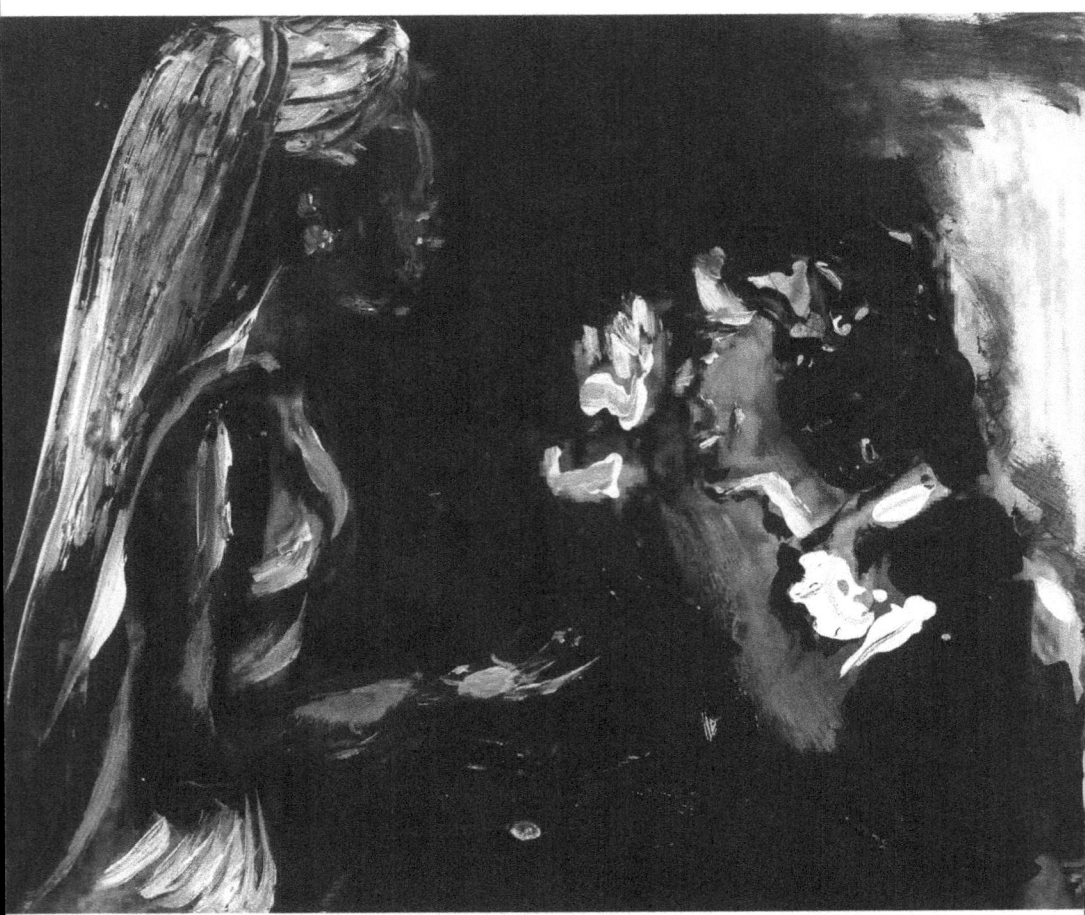

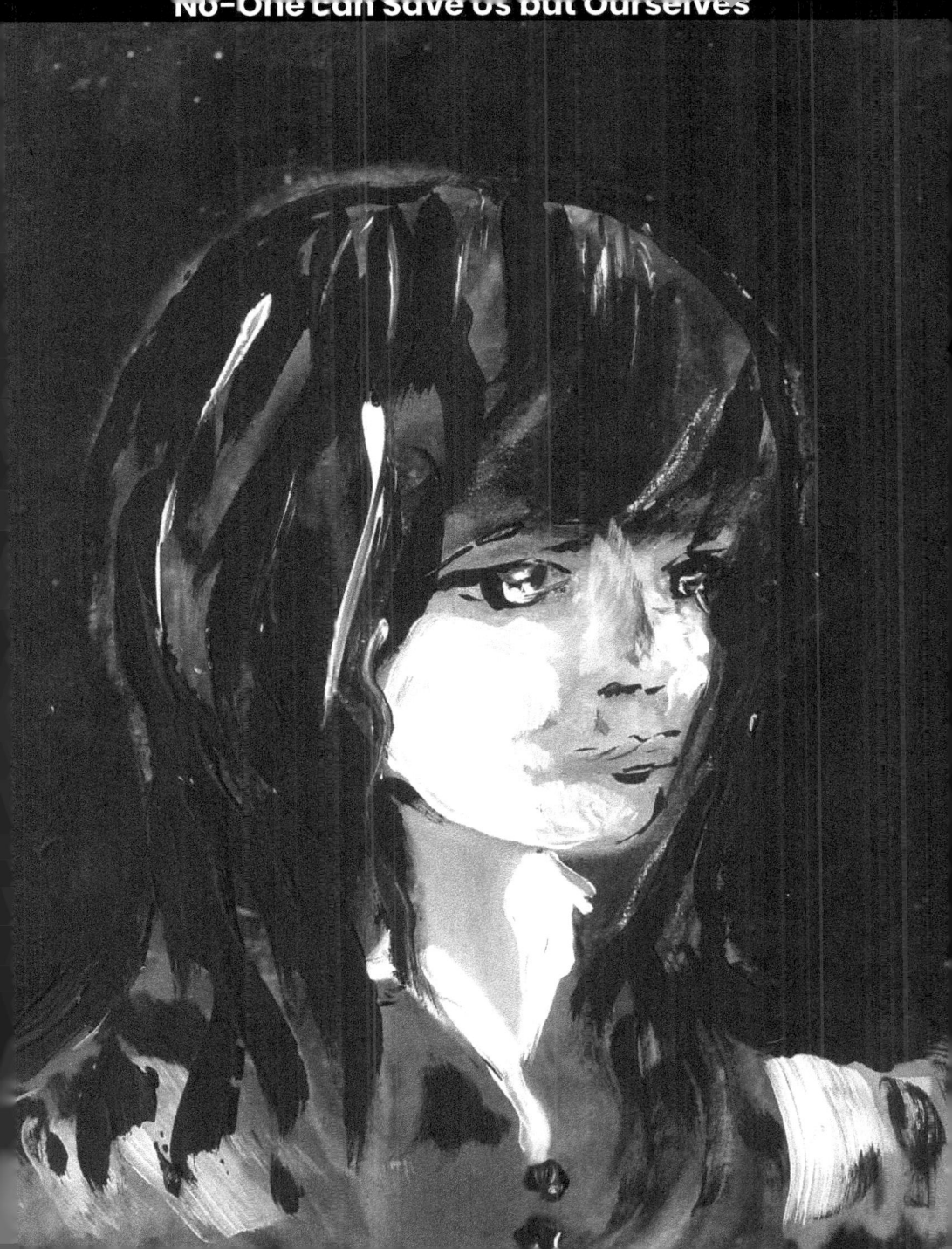

No-One Can Save Us but Ourselves

Be Where You Are or You Will Miss Your Life

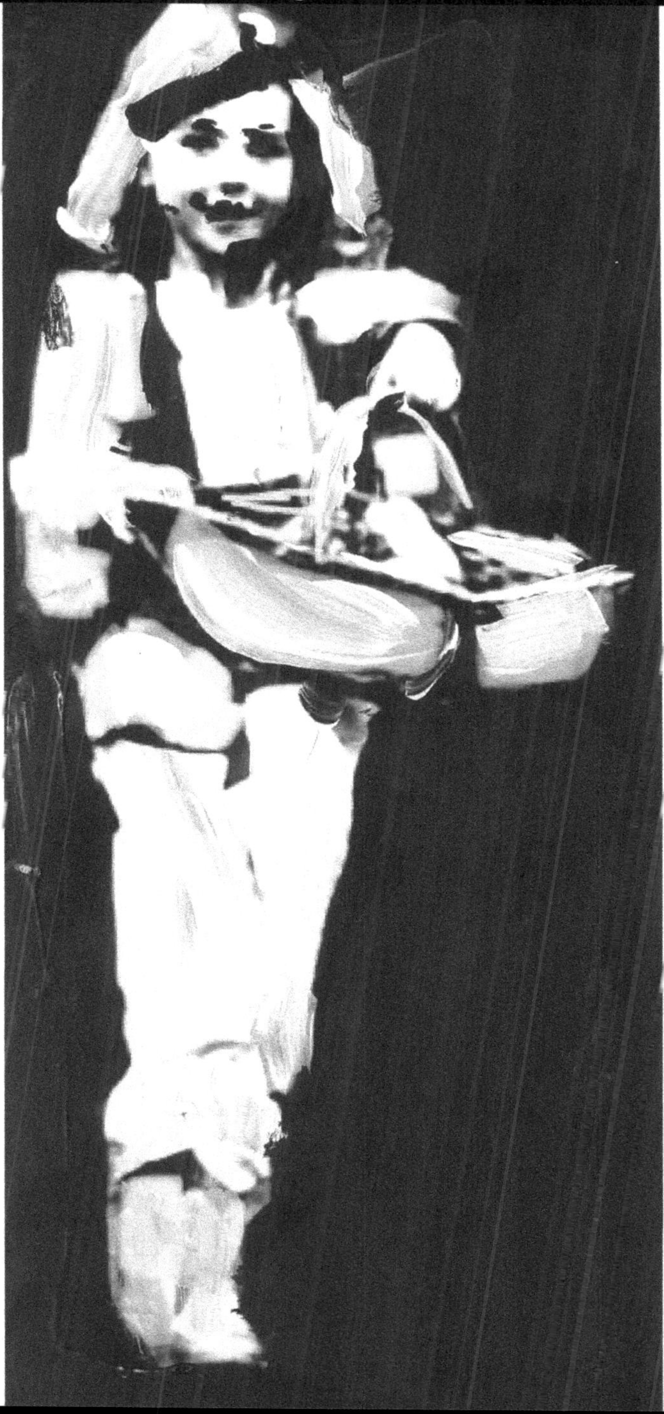

Like the Moon; Shine

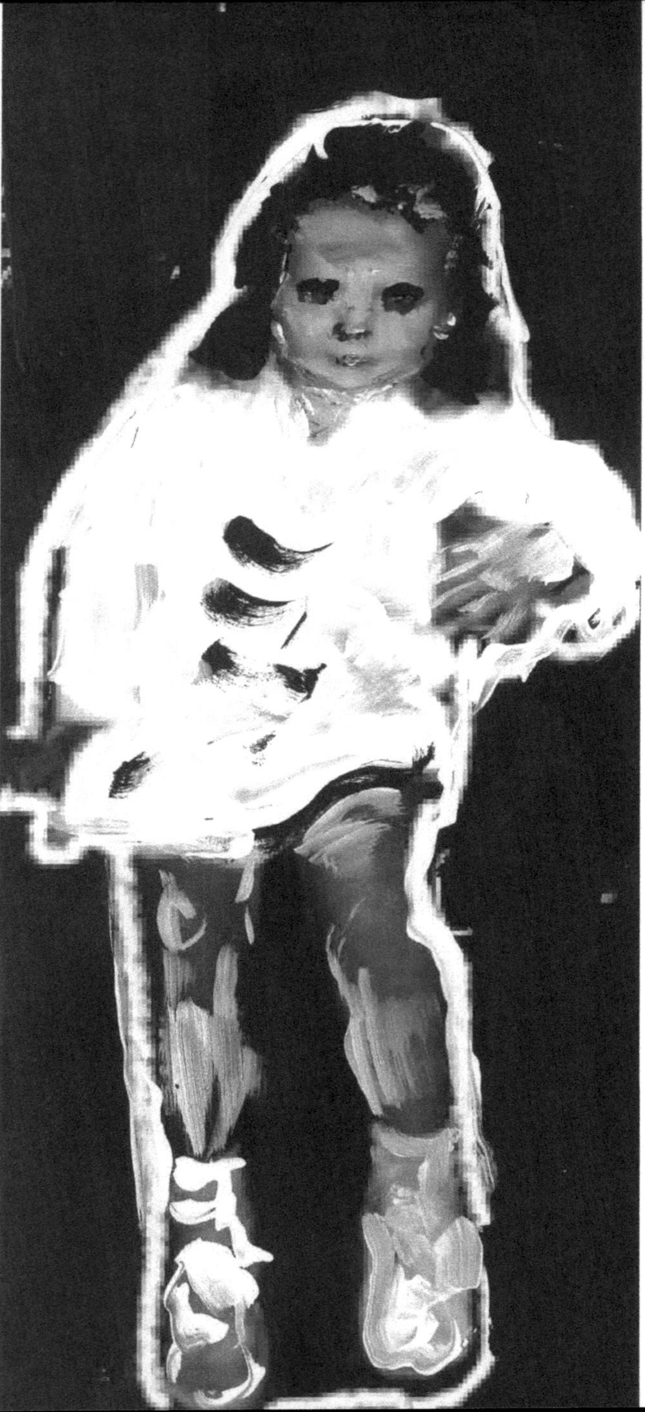

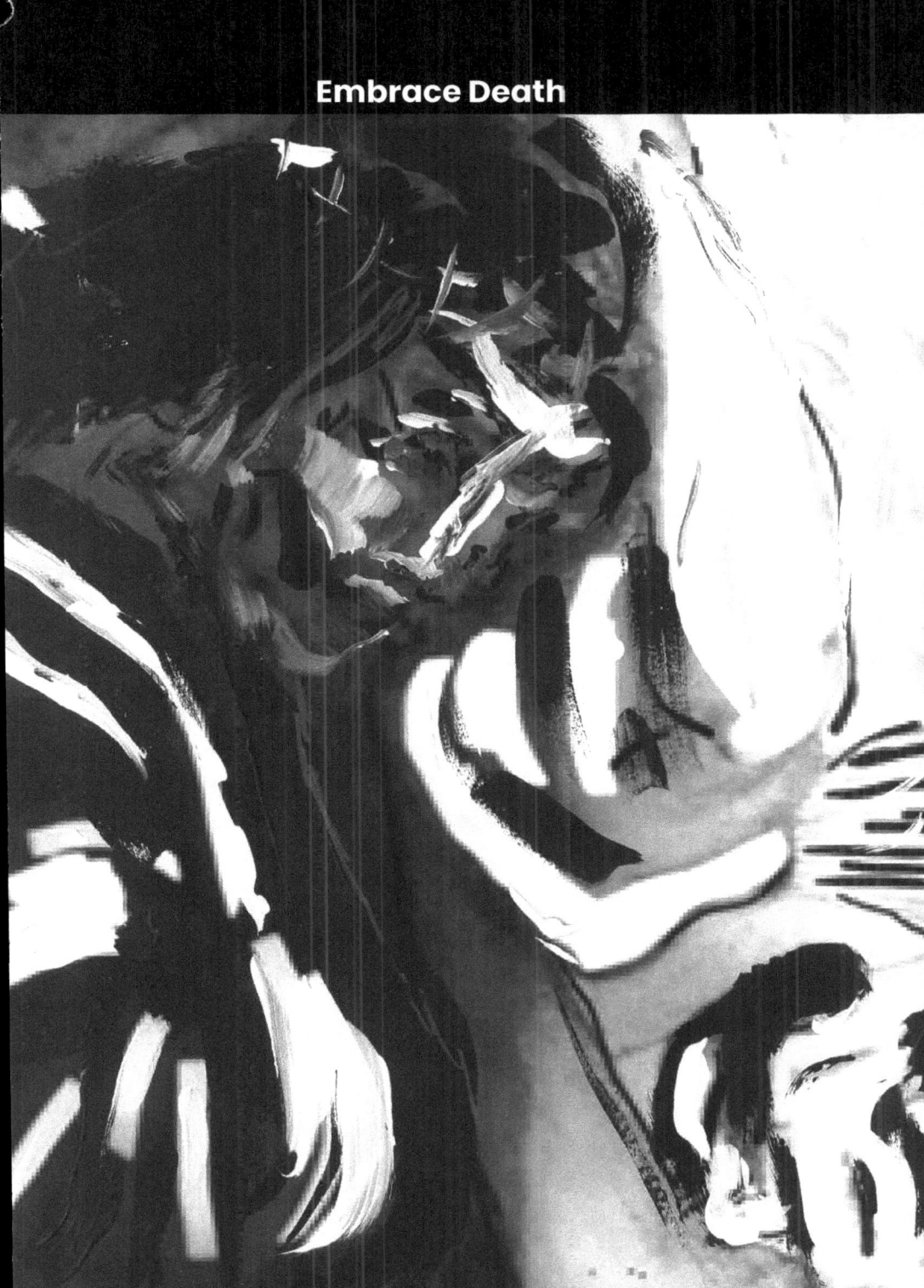

Embrace Death

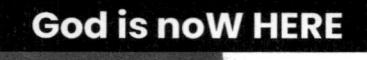

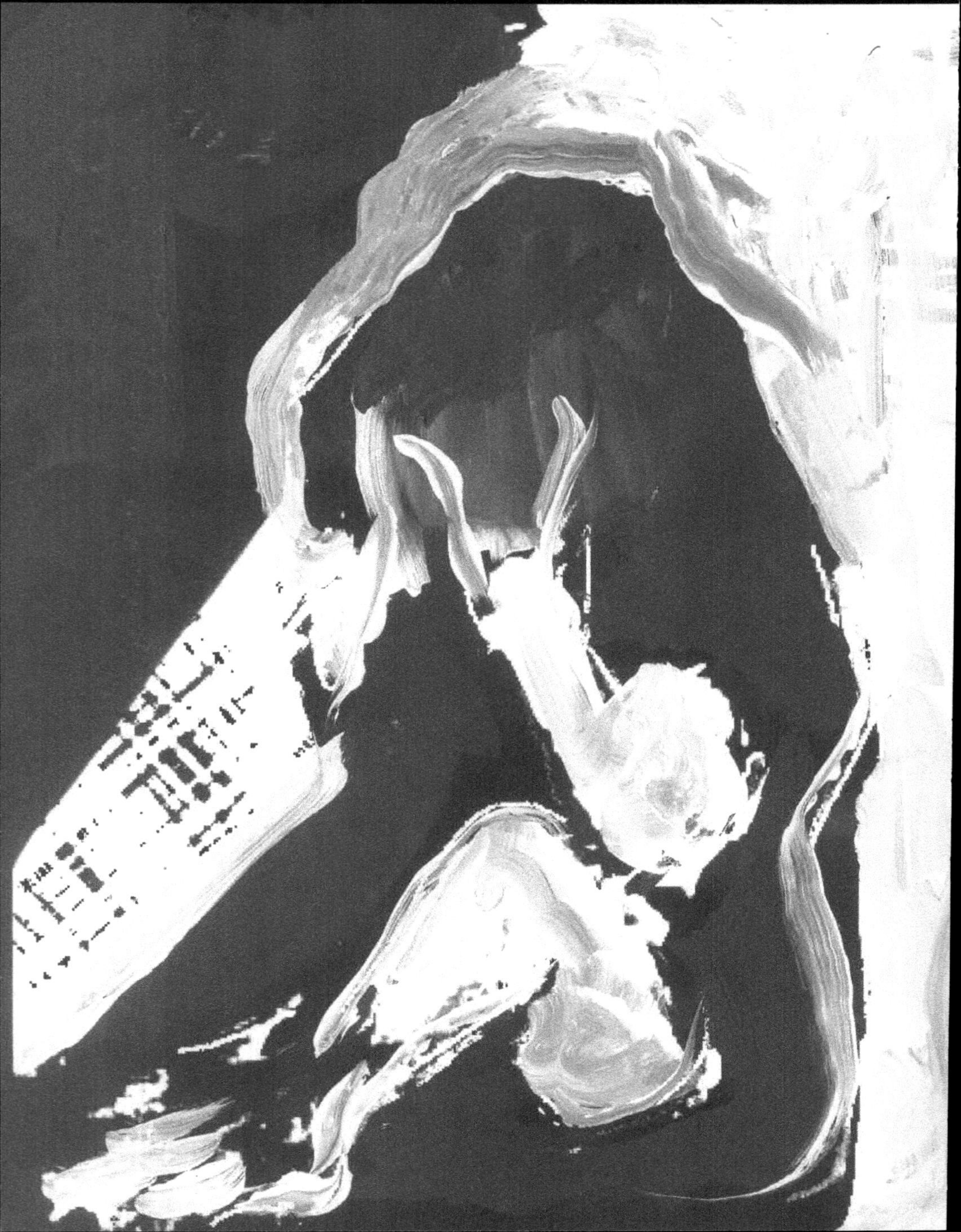

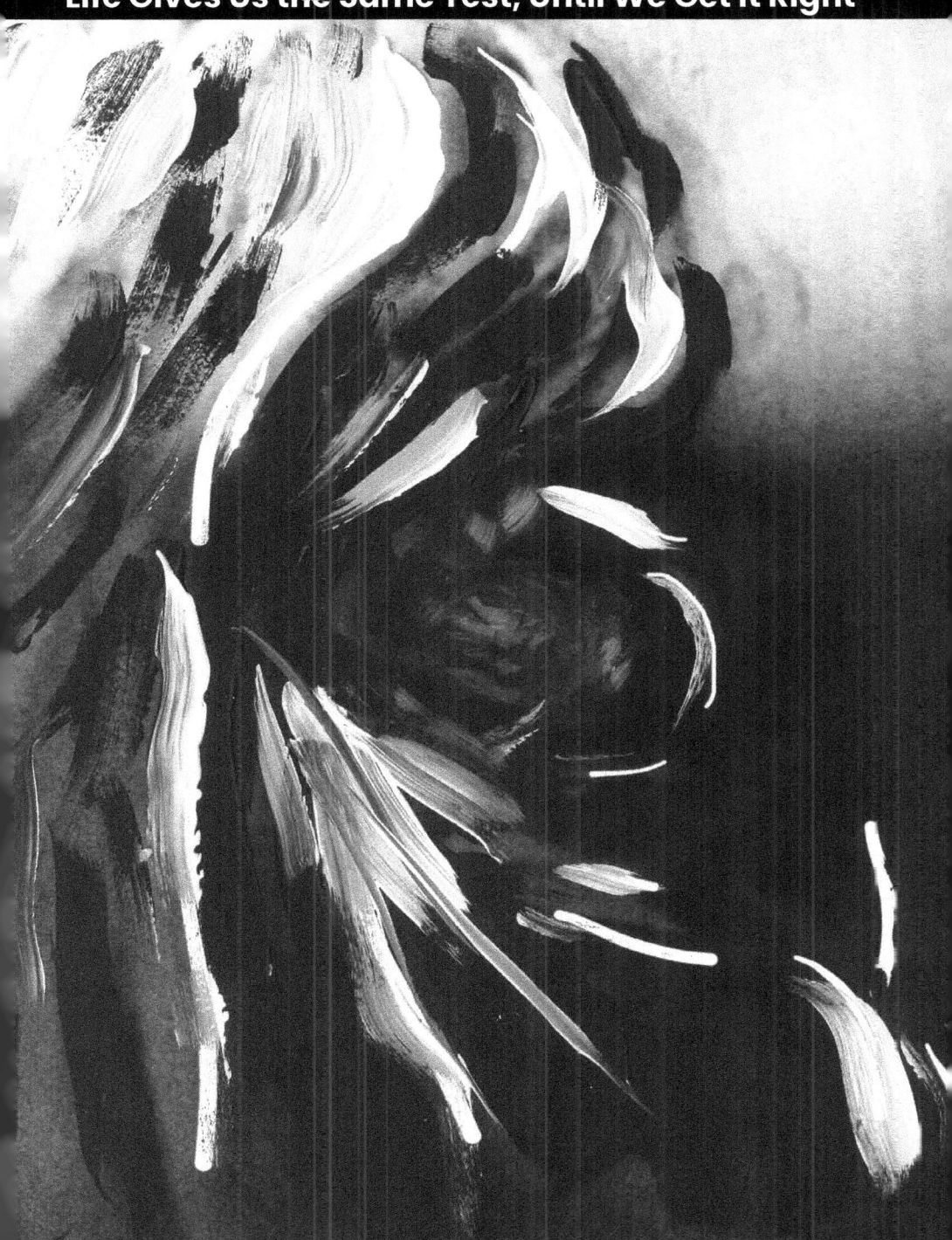

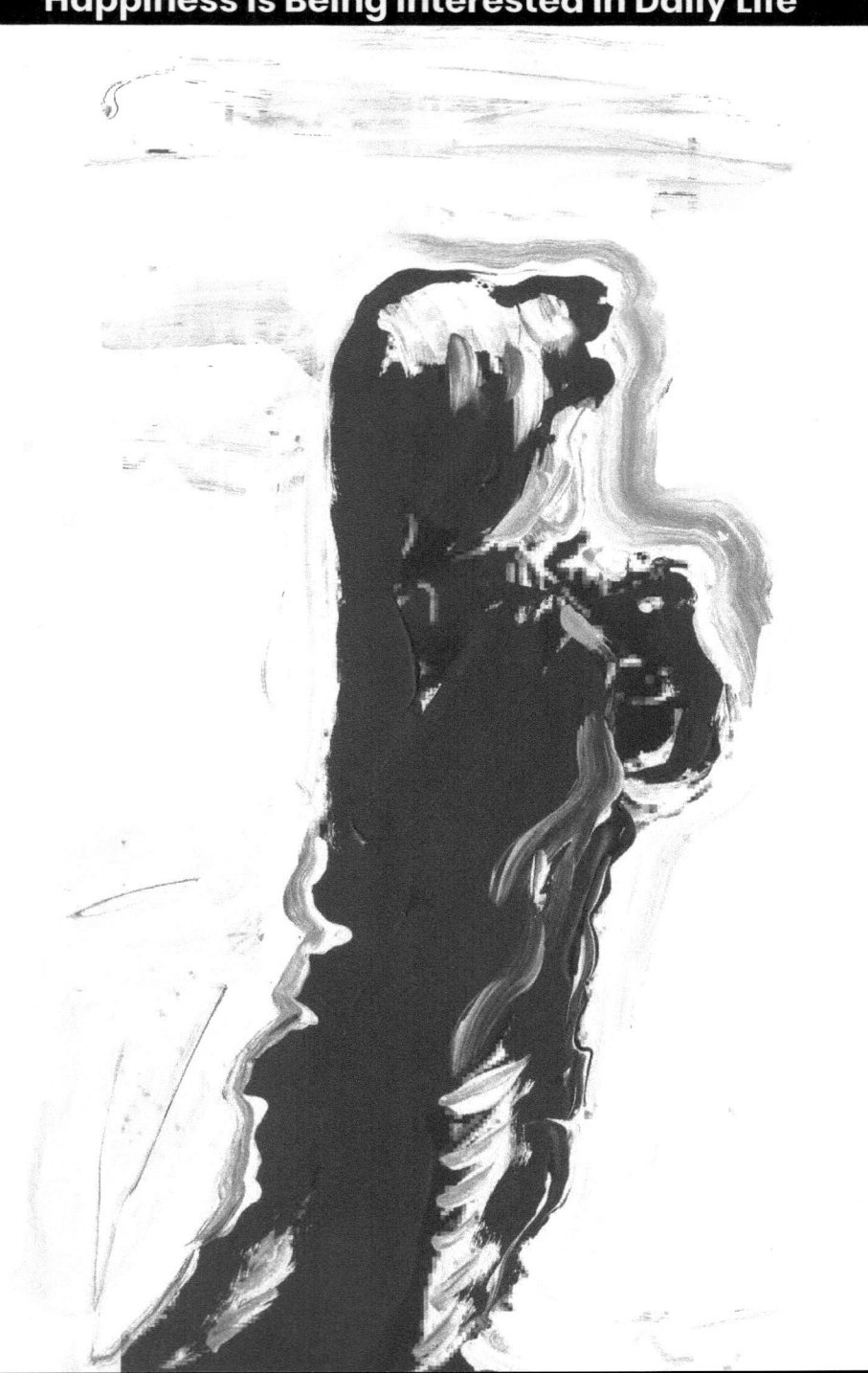

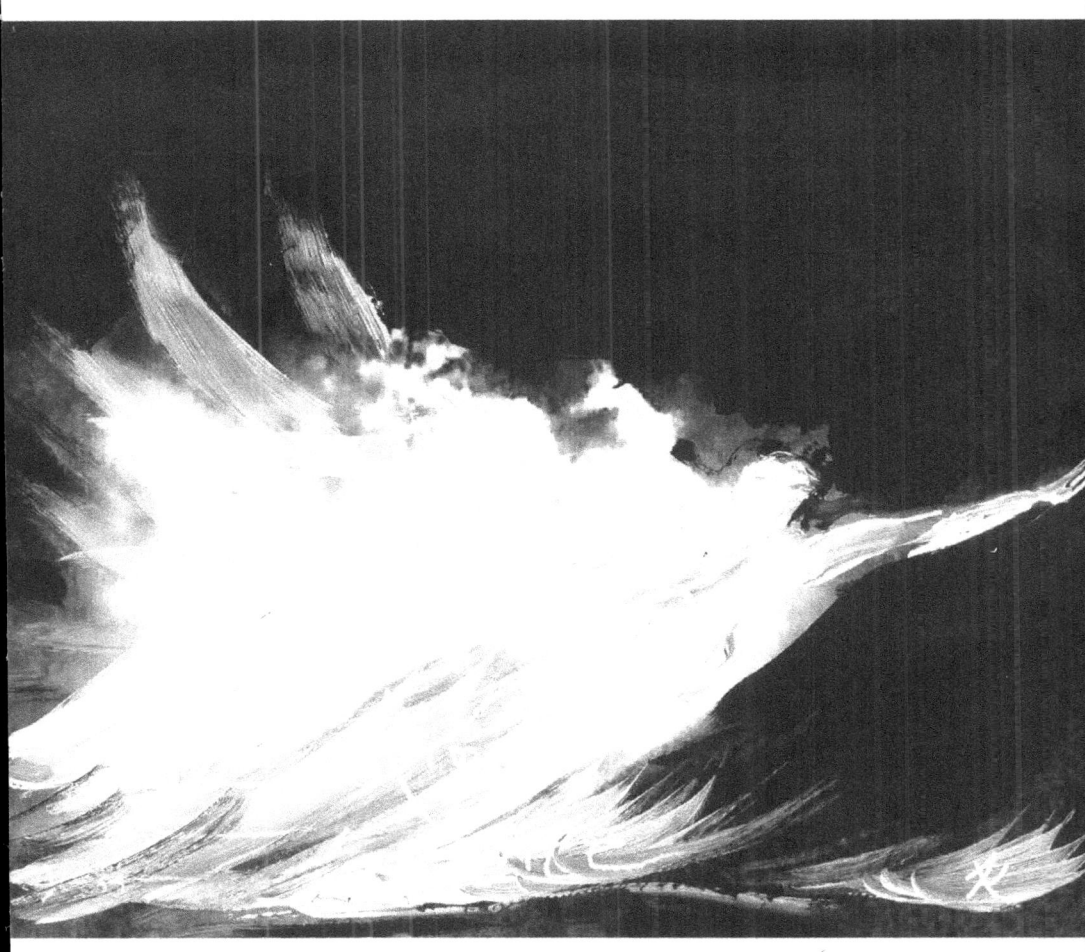

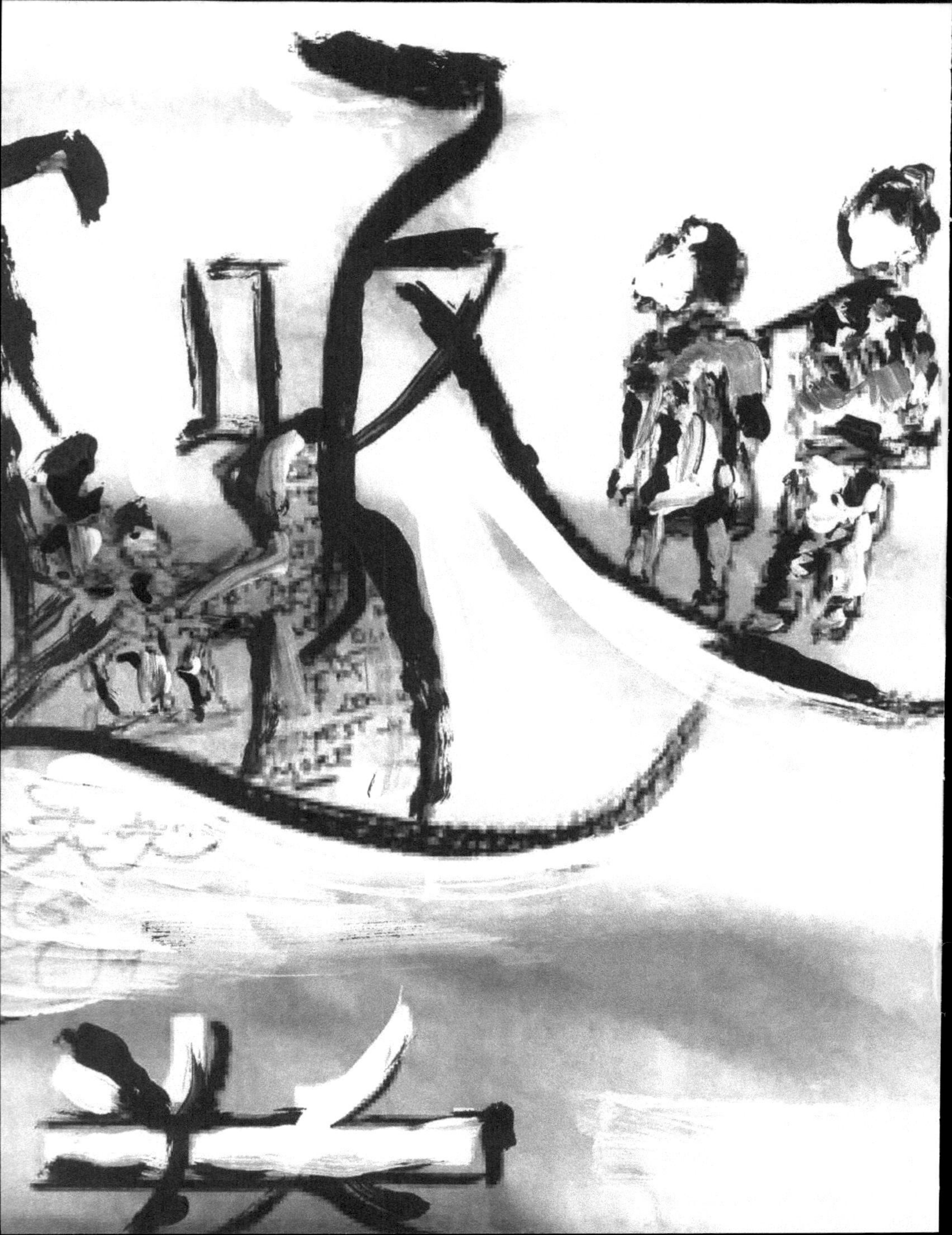

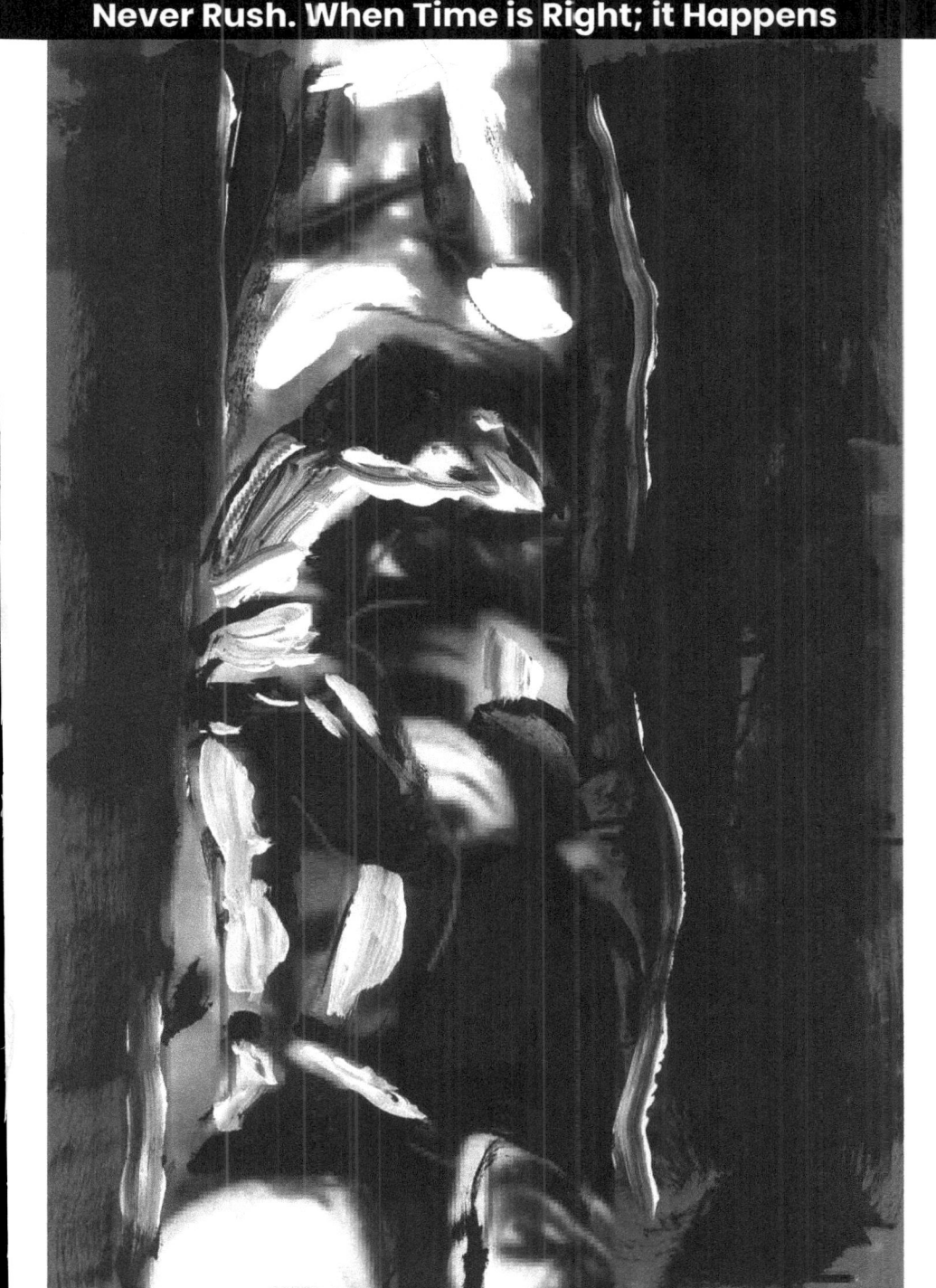

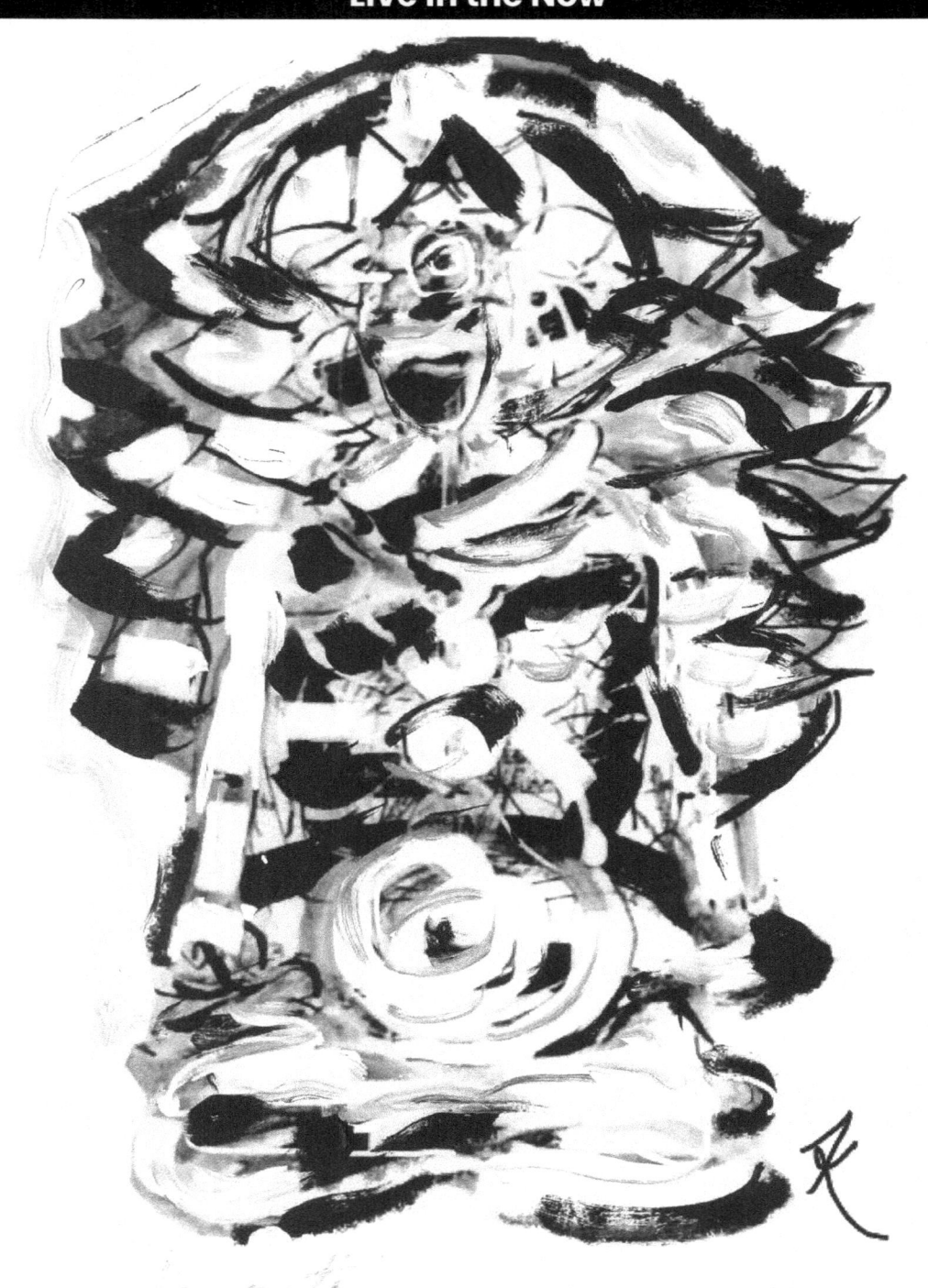

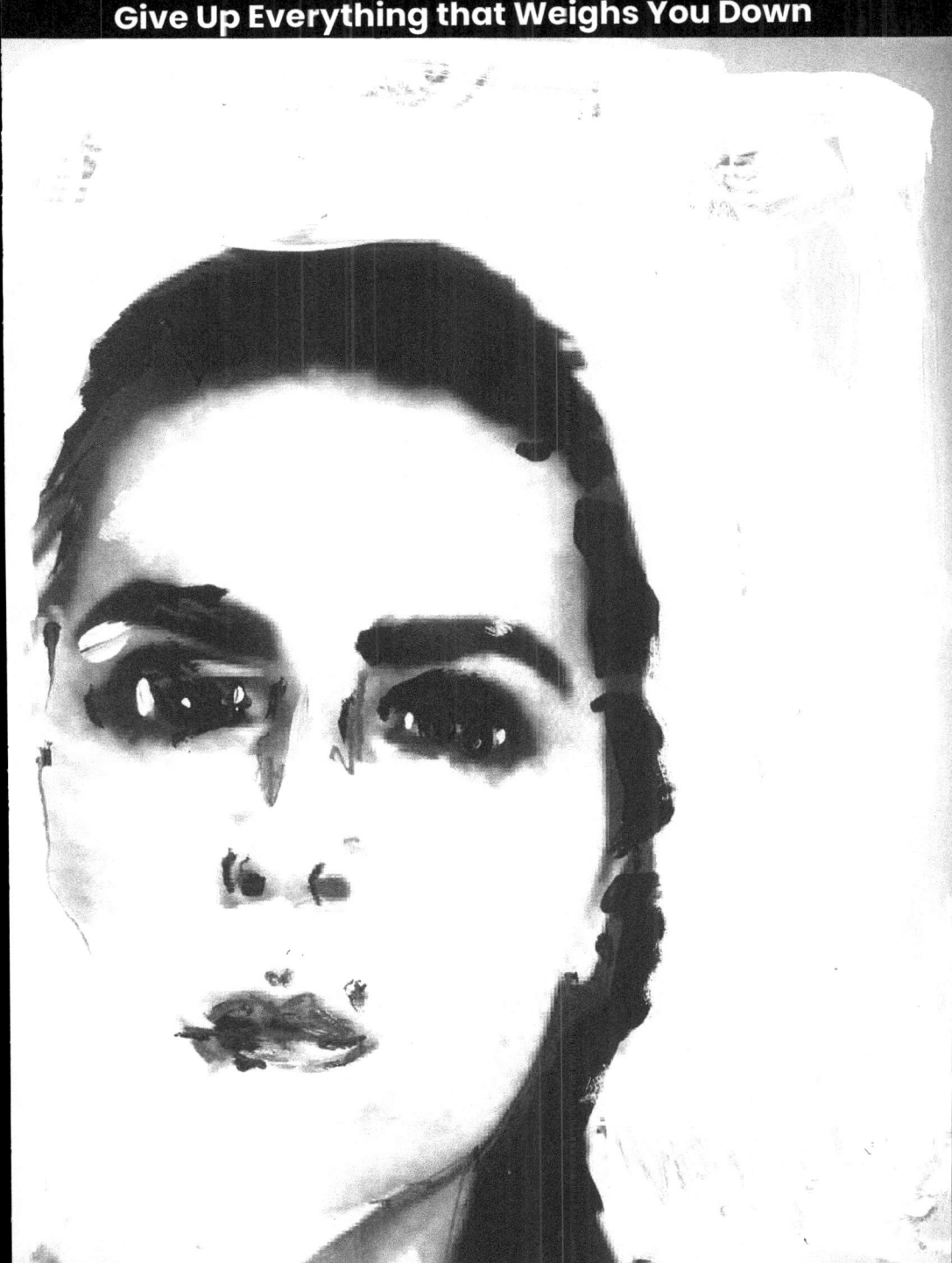

When Ego Dies, The Soul Awakes

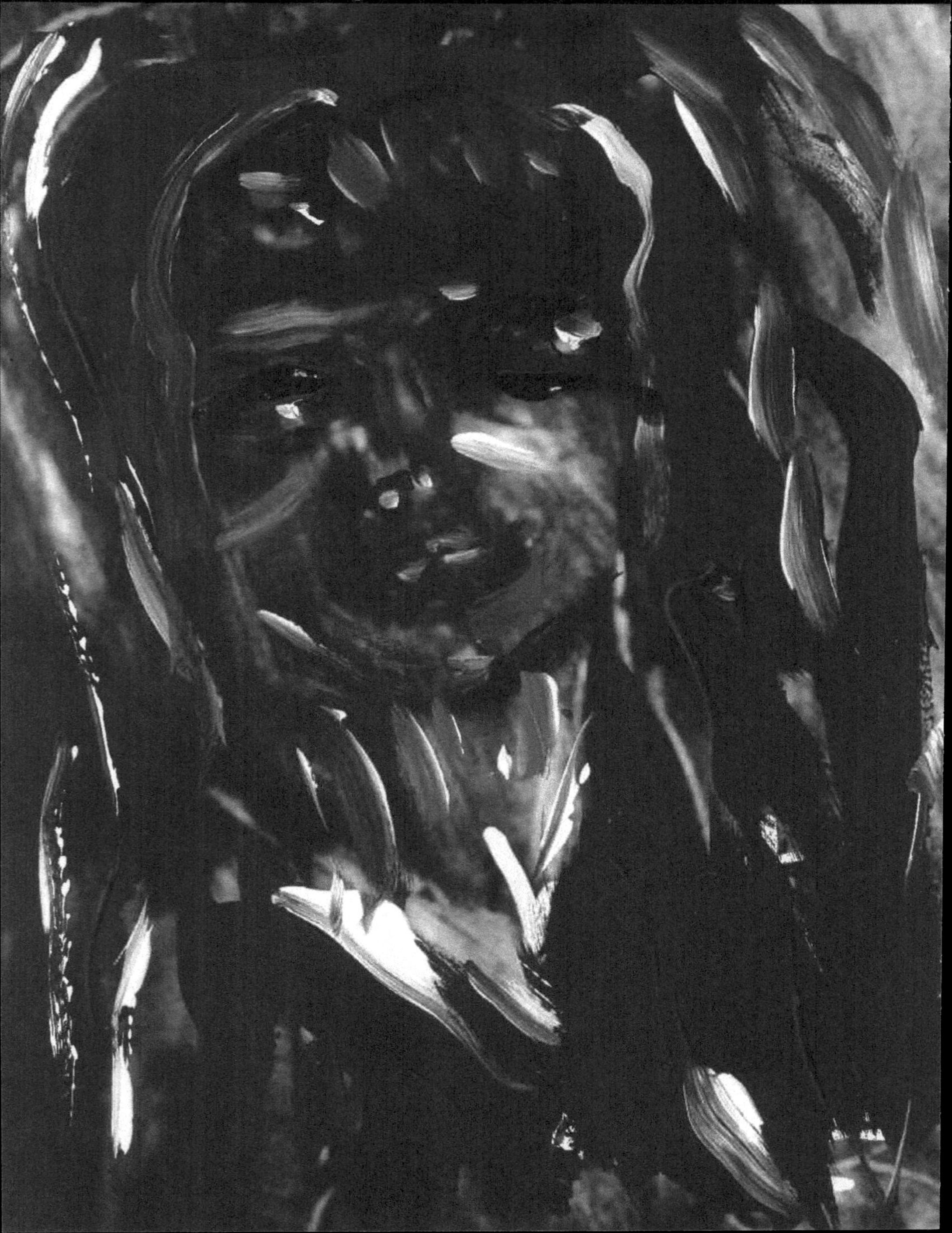

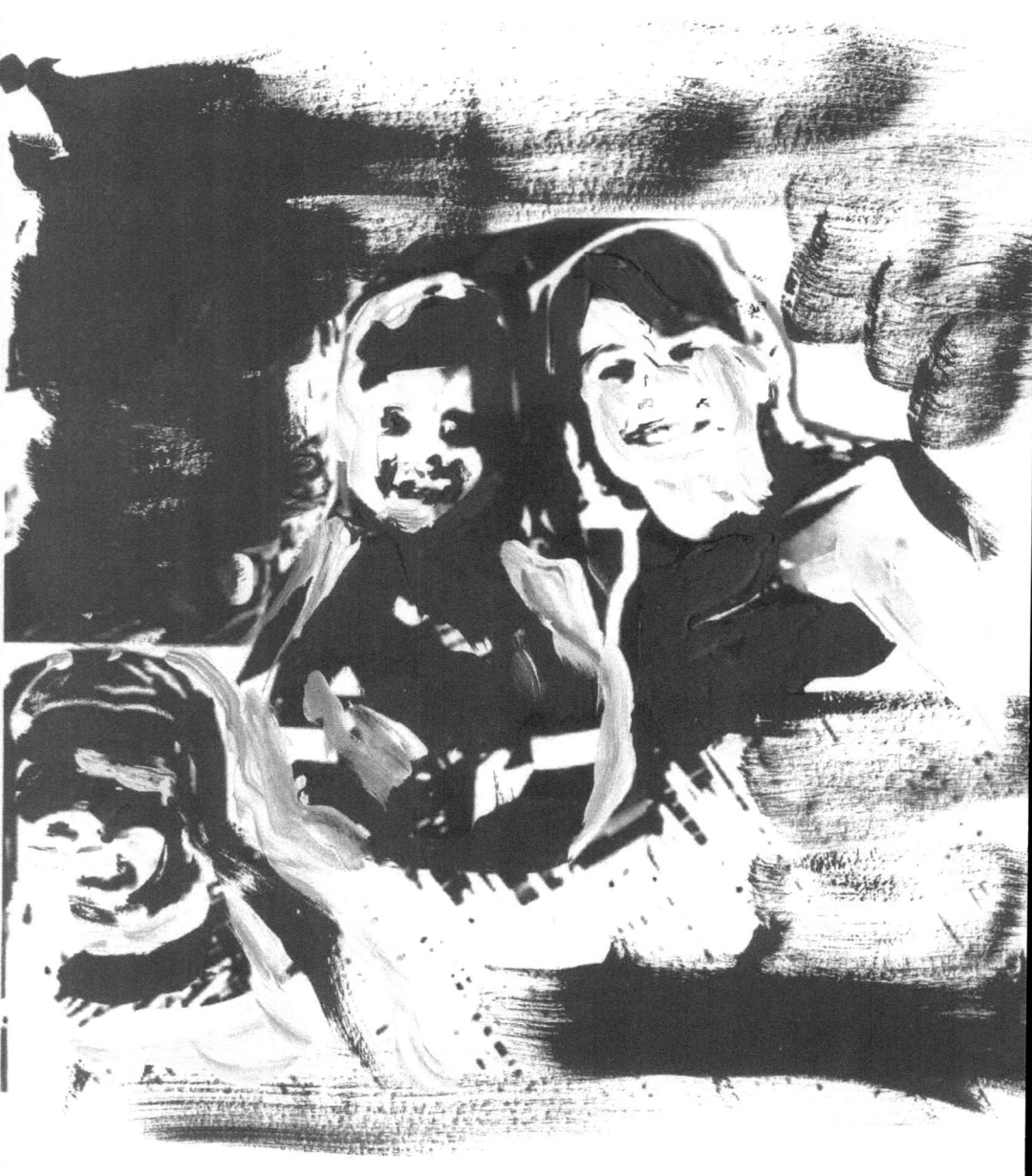

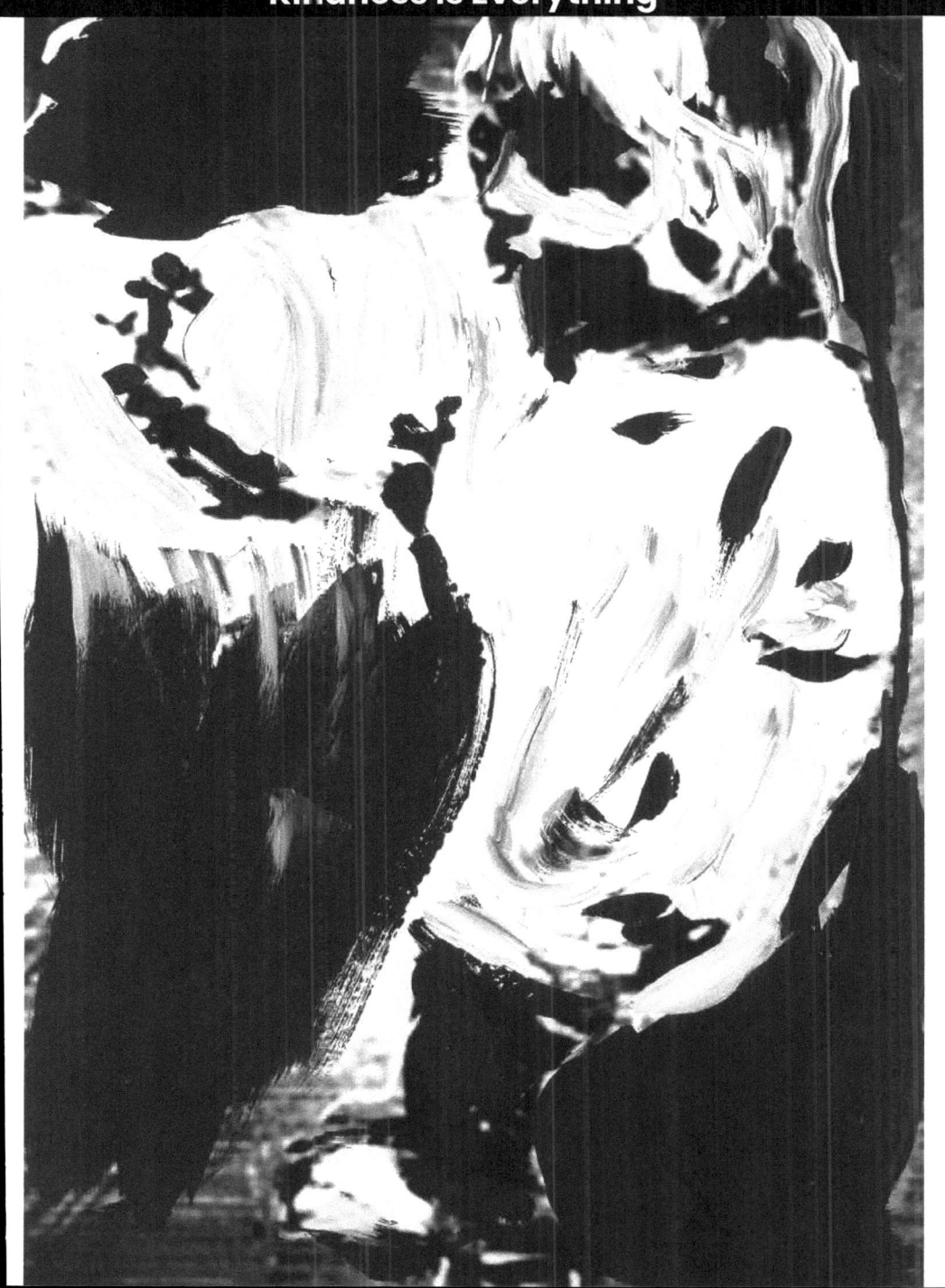

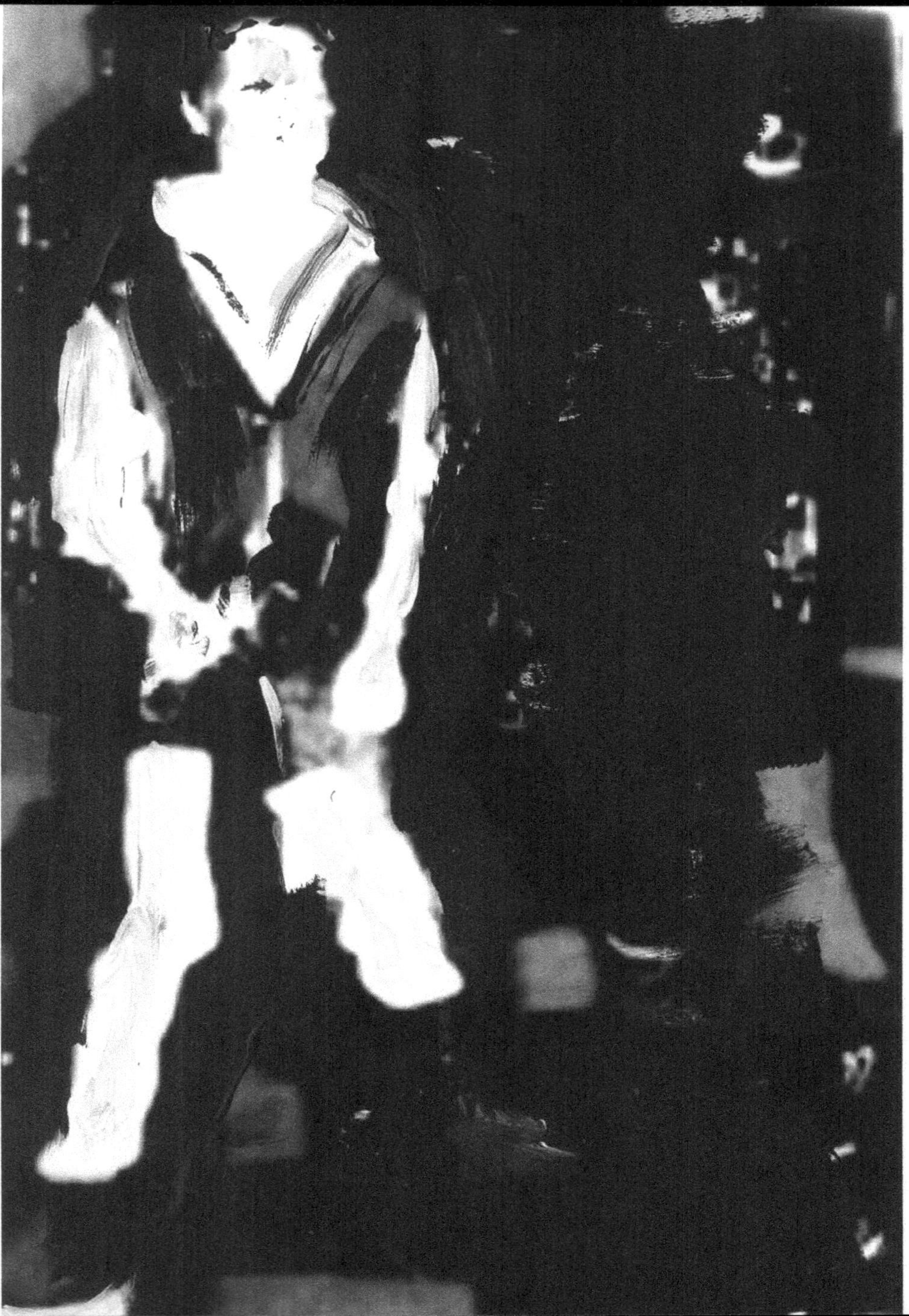

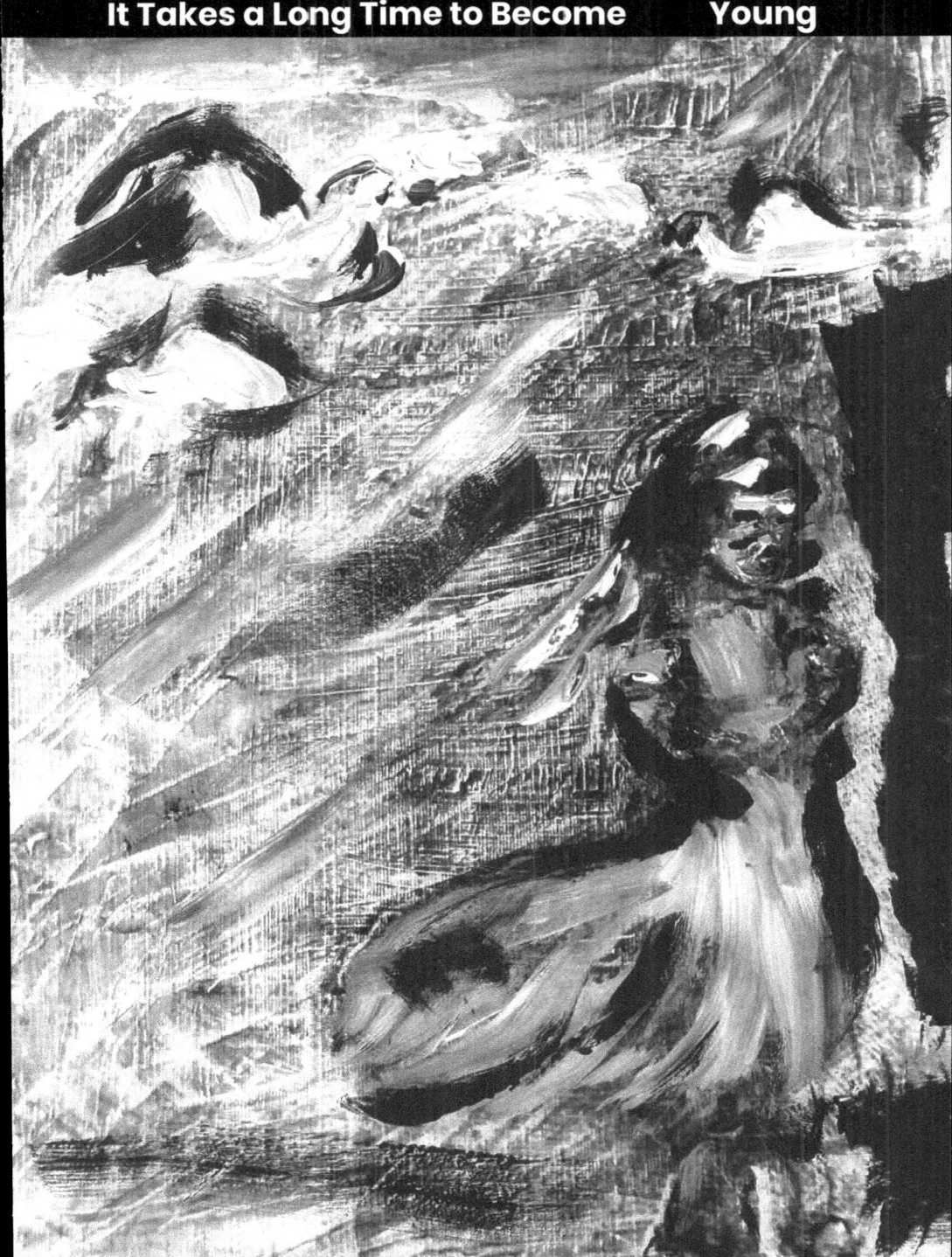

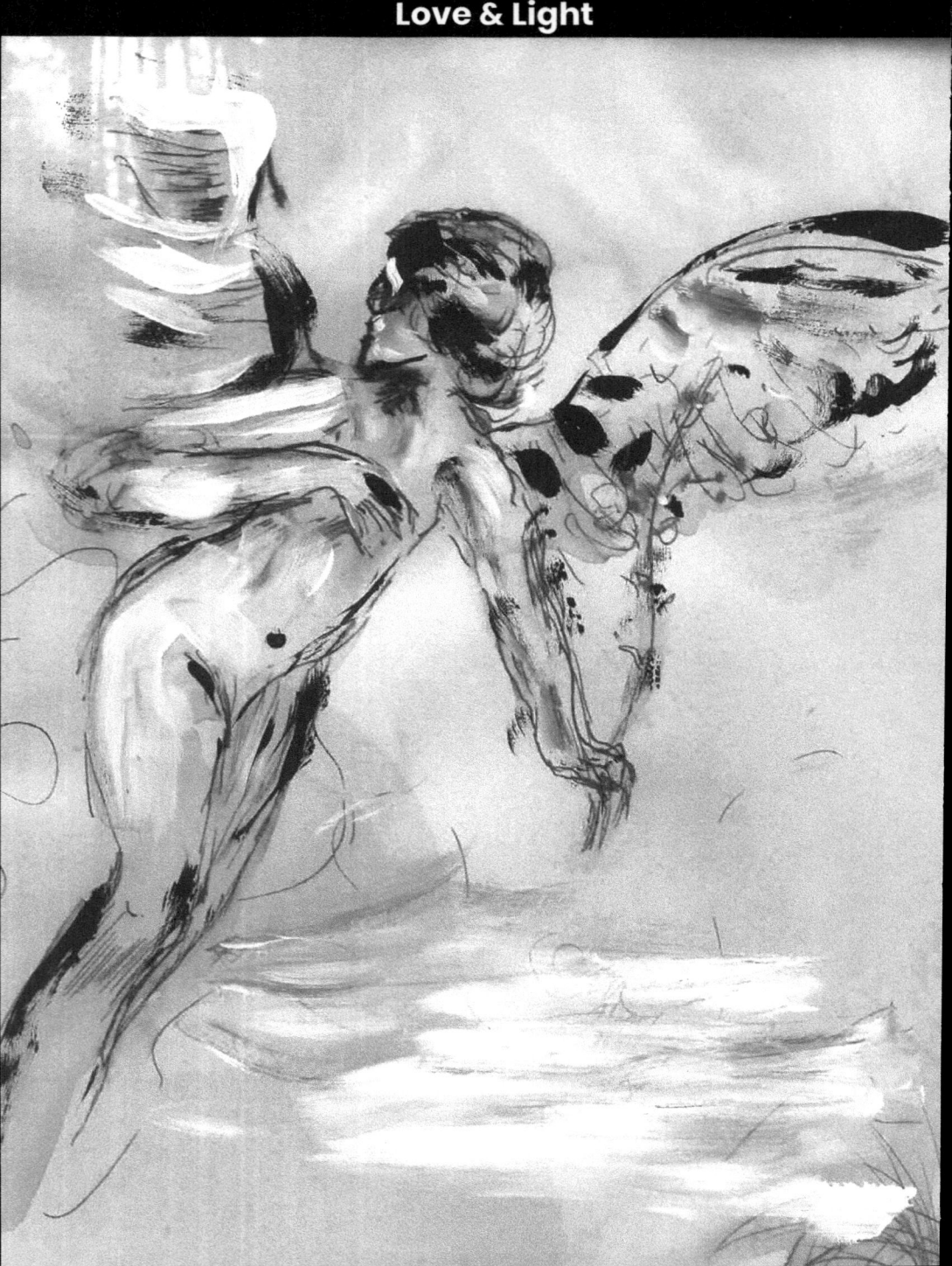

Not Getting What You Want is Lucky, Sometimes

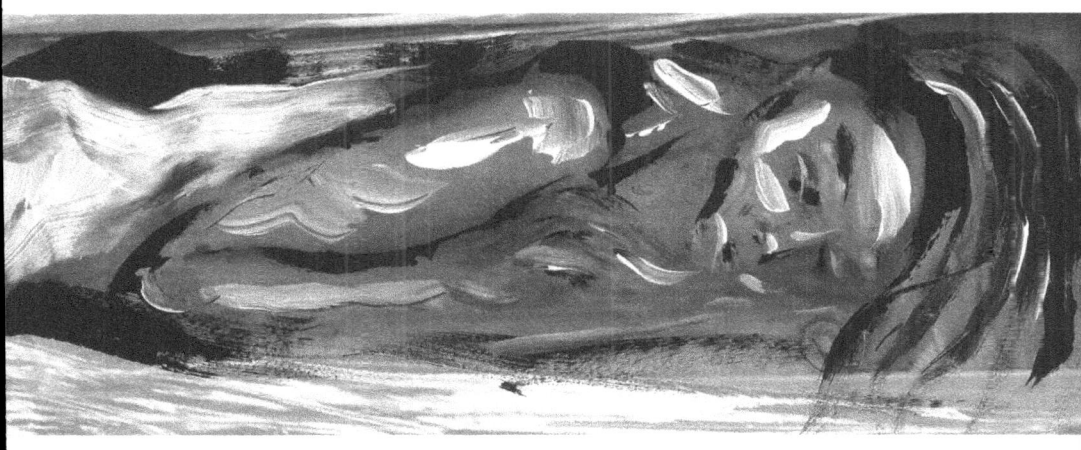

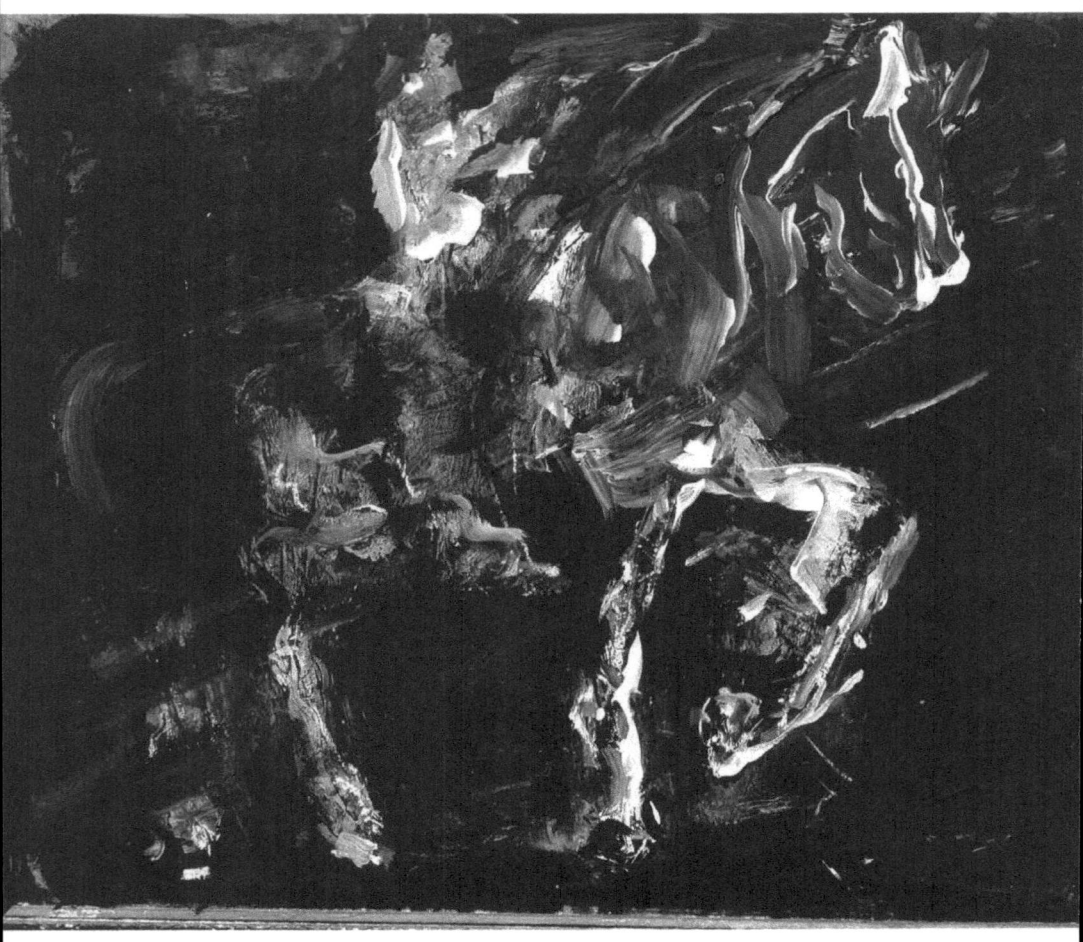

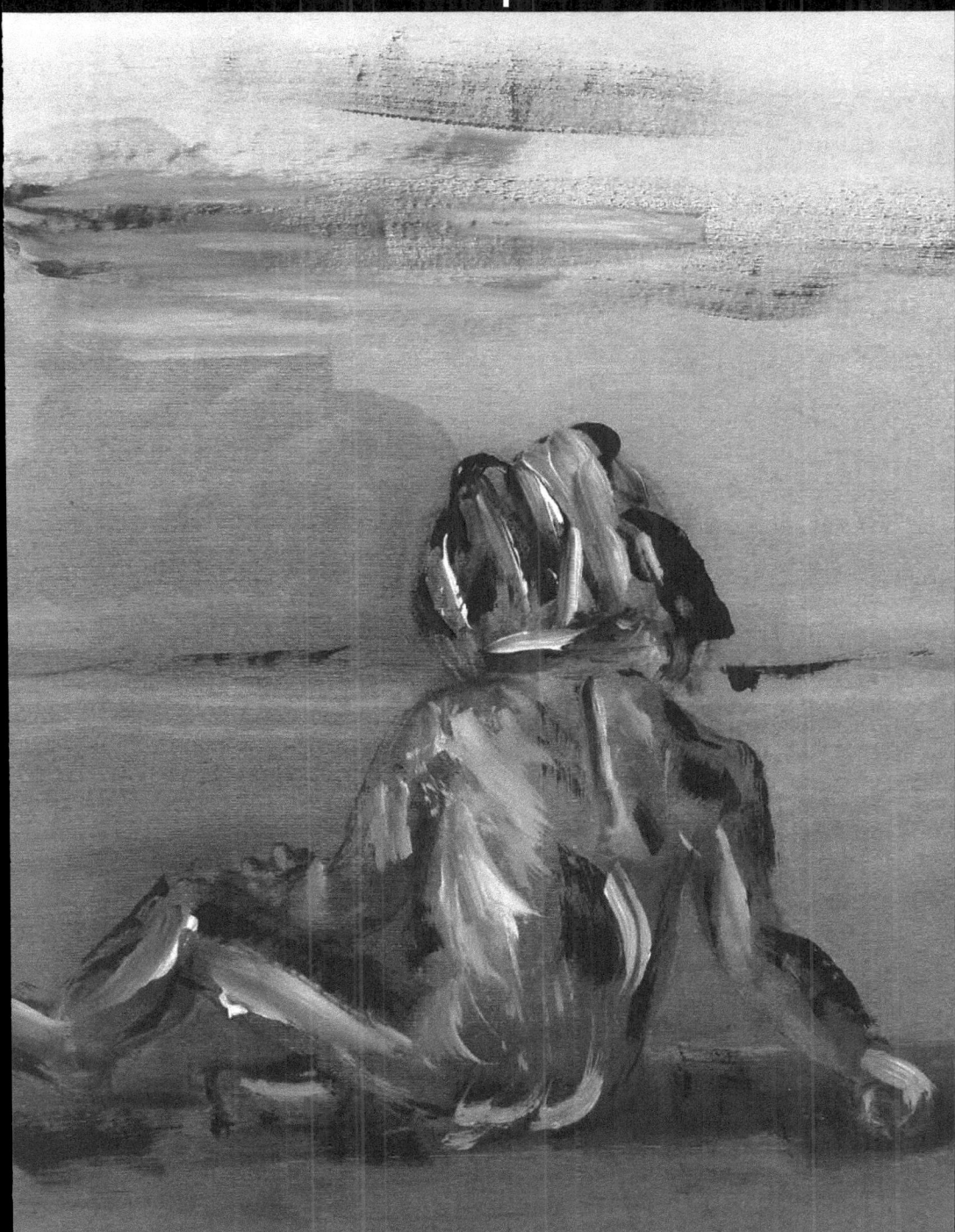

No-One can Replace You

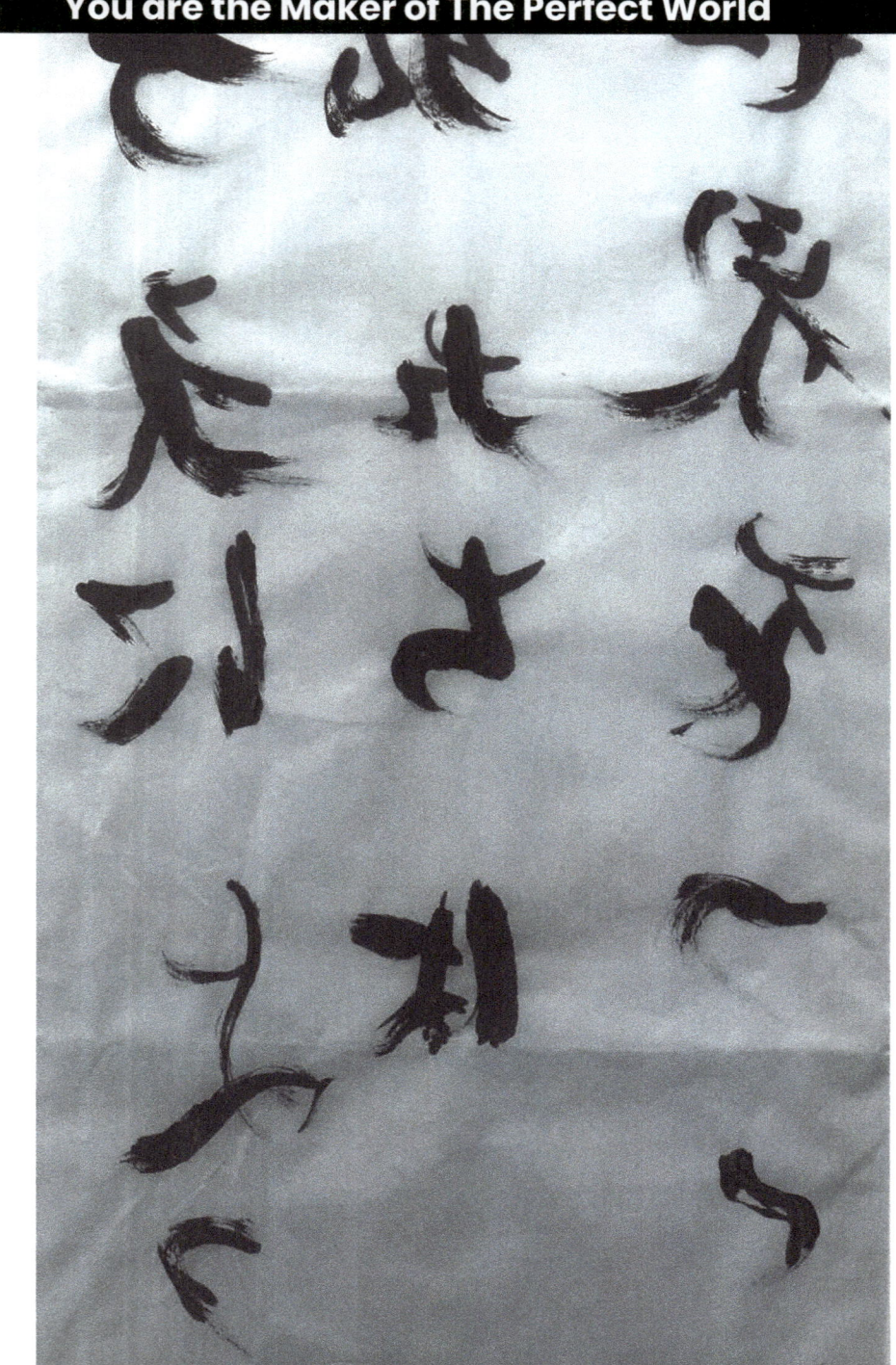

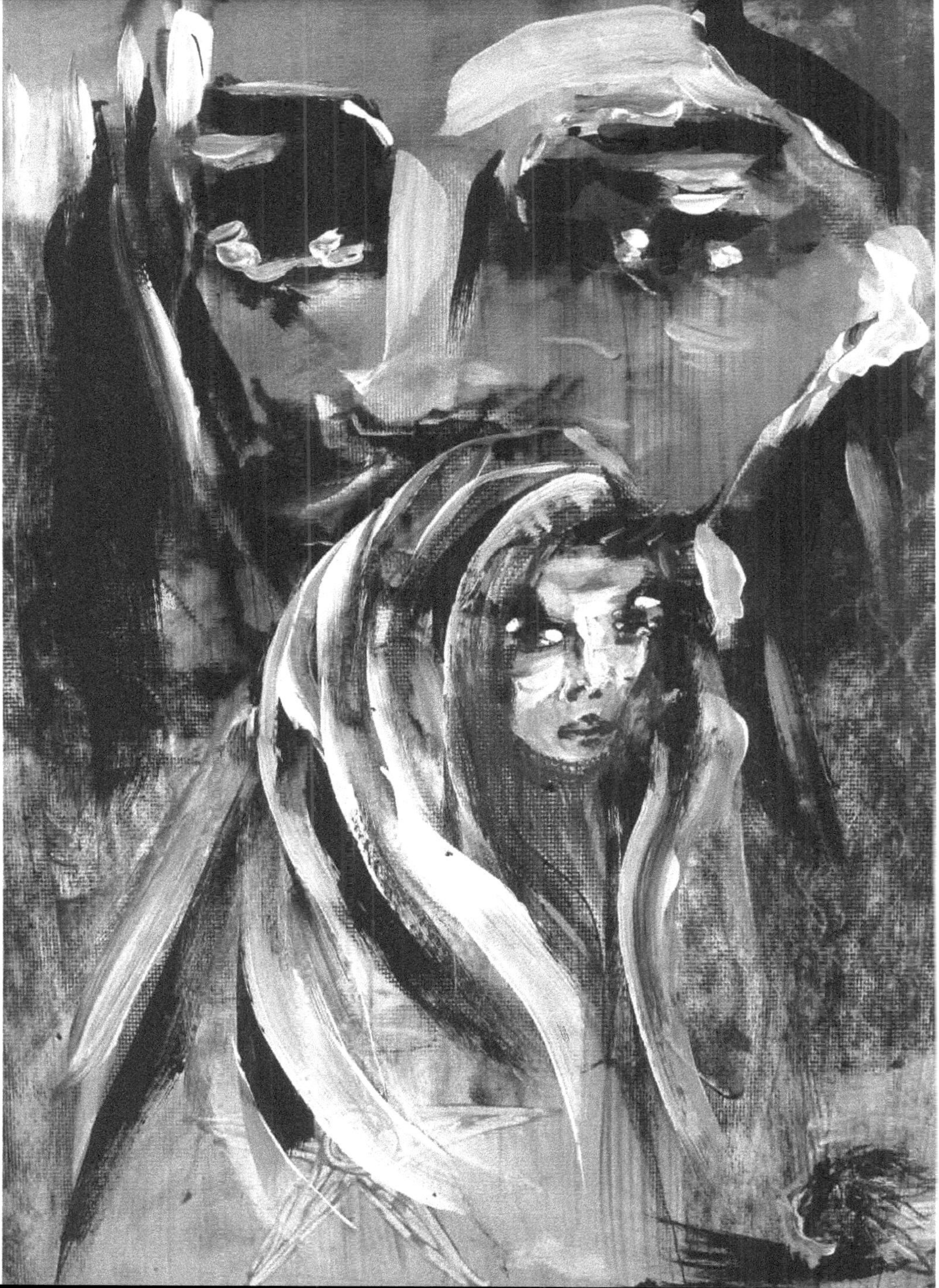

Nothing can Erase Your Good Deeds

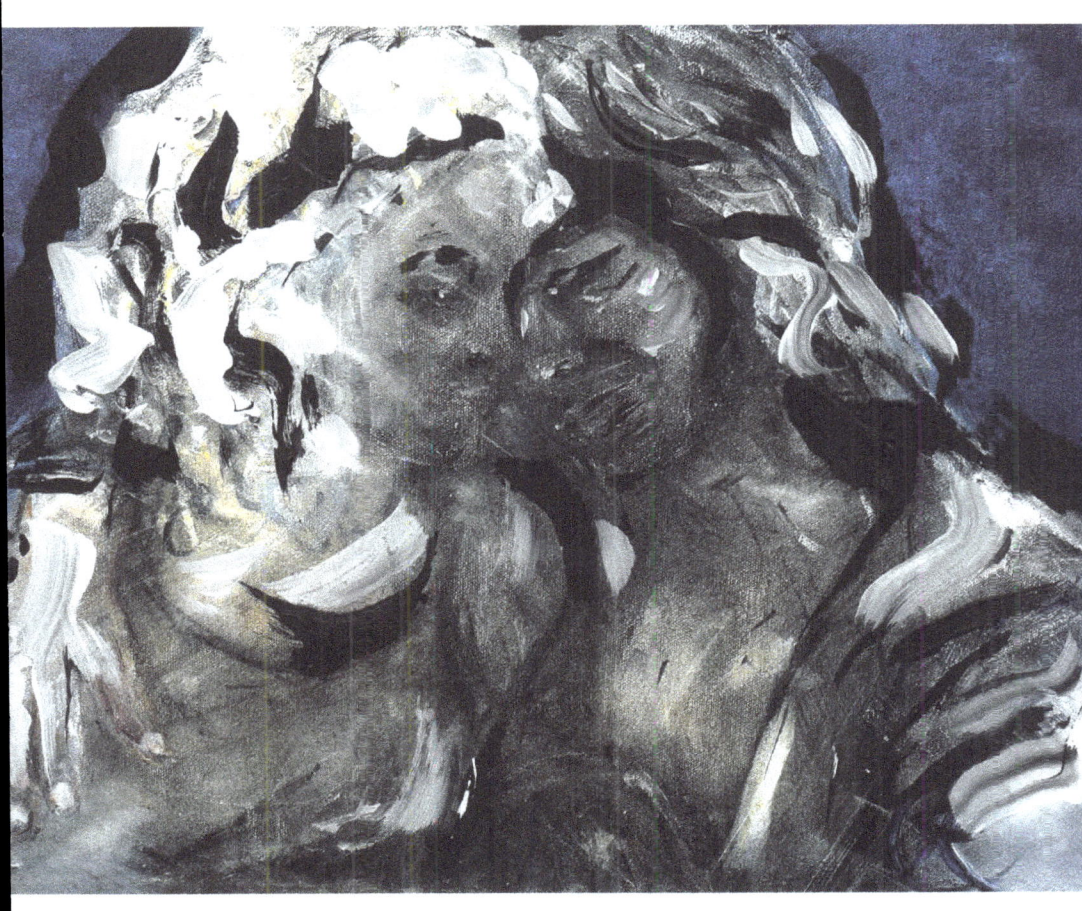

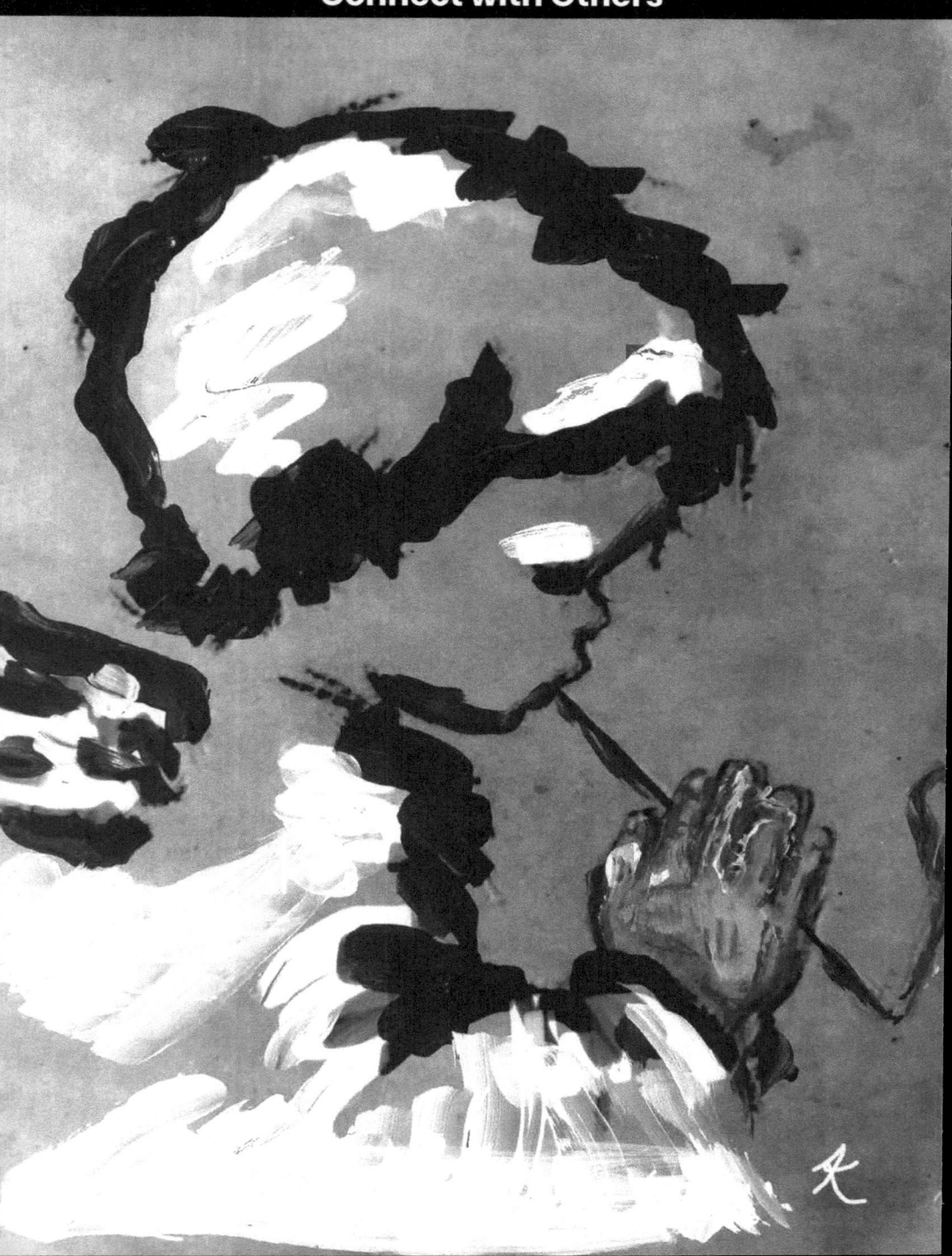

Loose your Looks, but Not your Sense of Humour

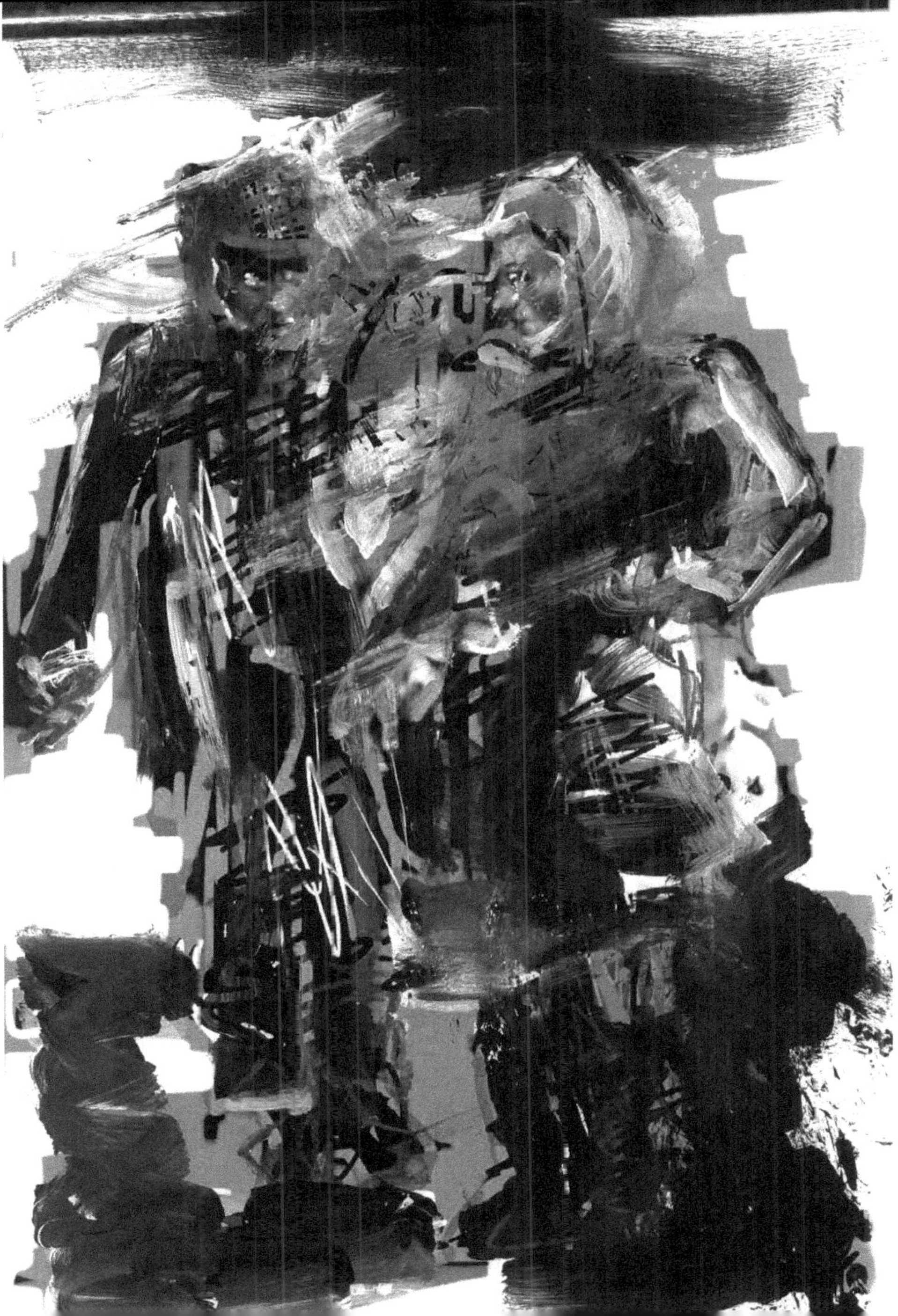

Better to Travel Alone than with a Fool

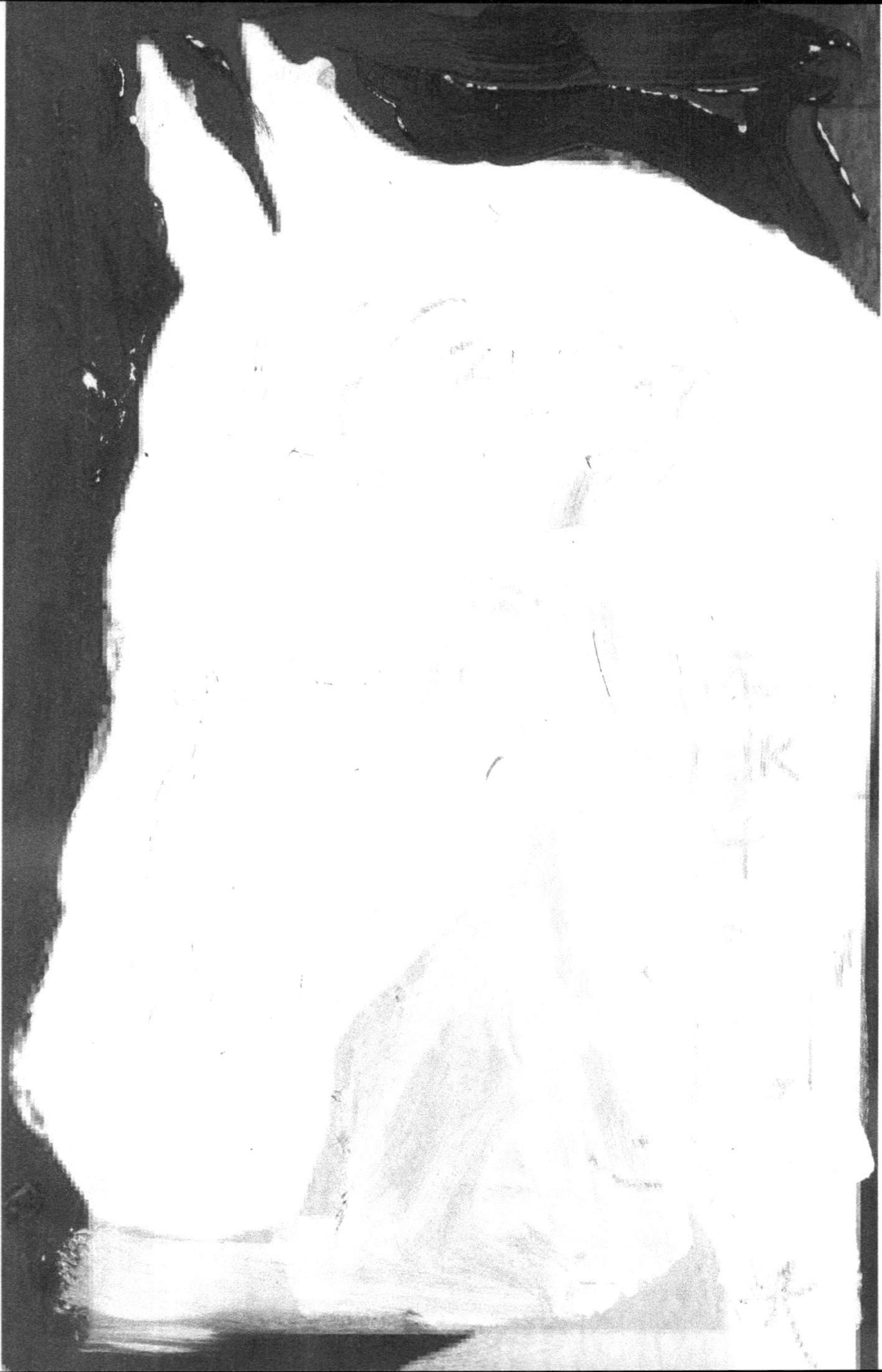

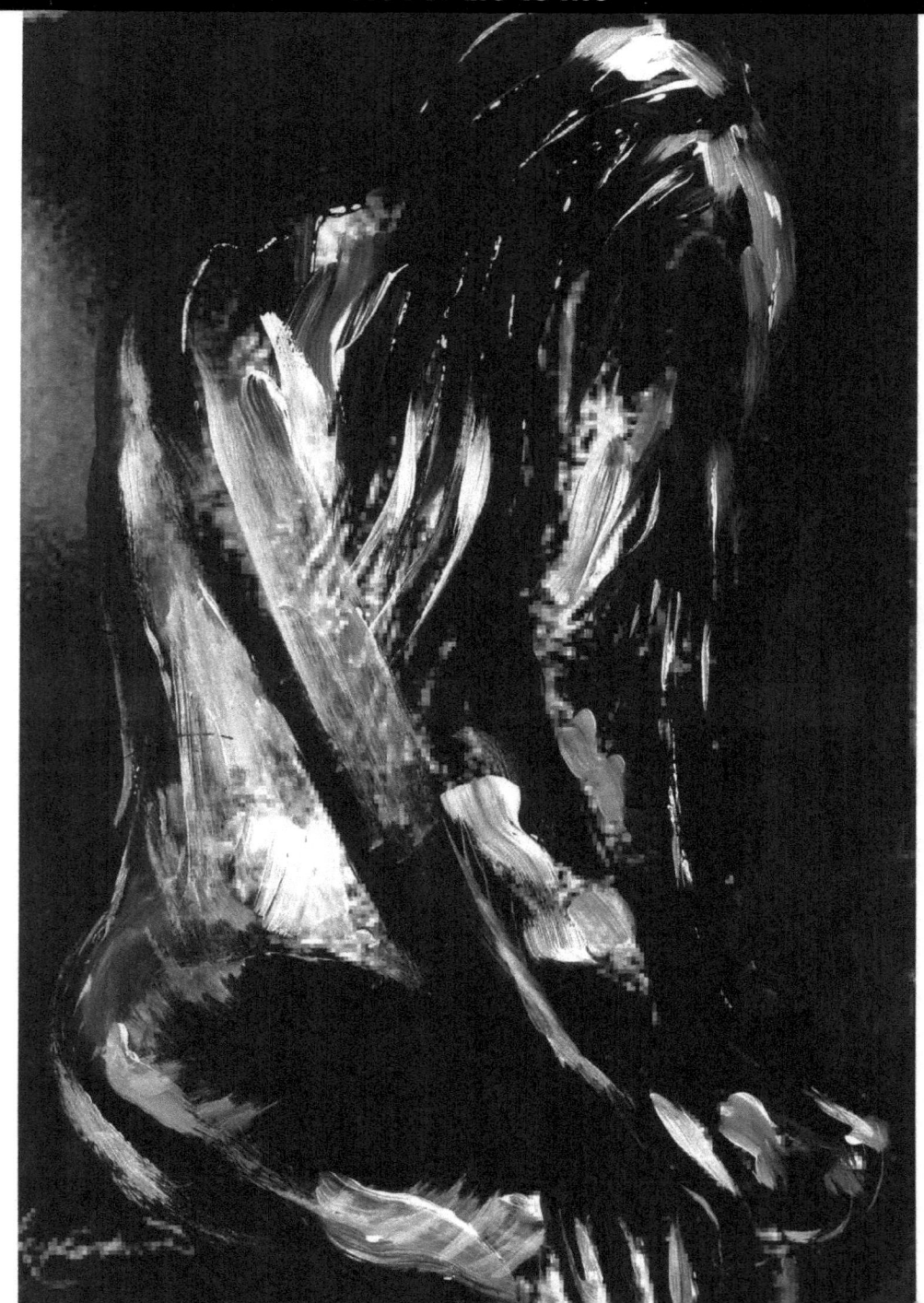

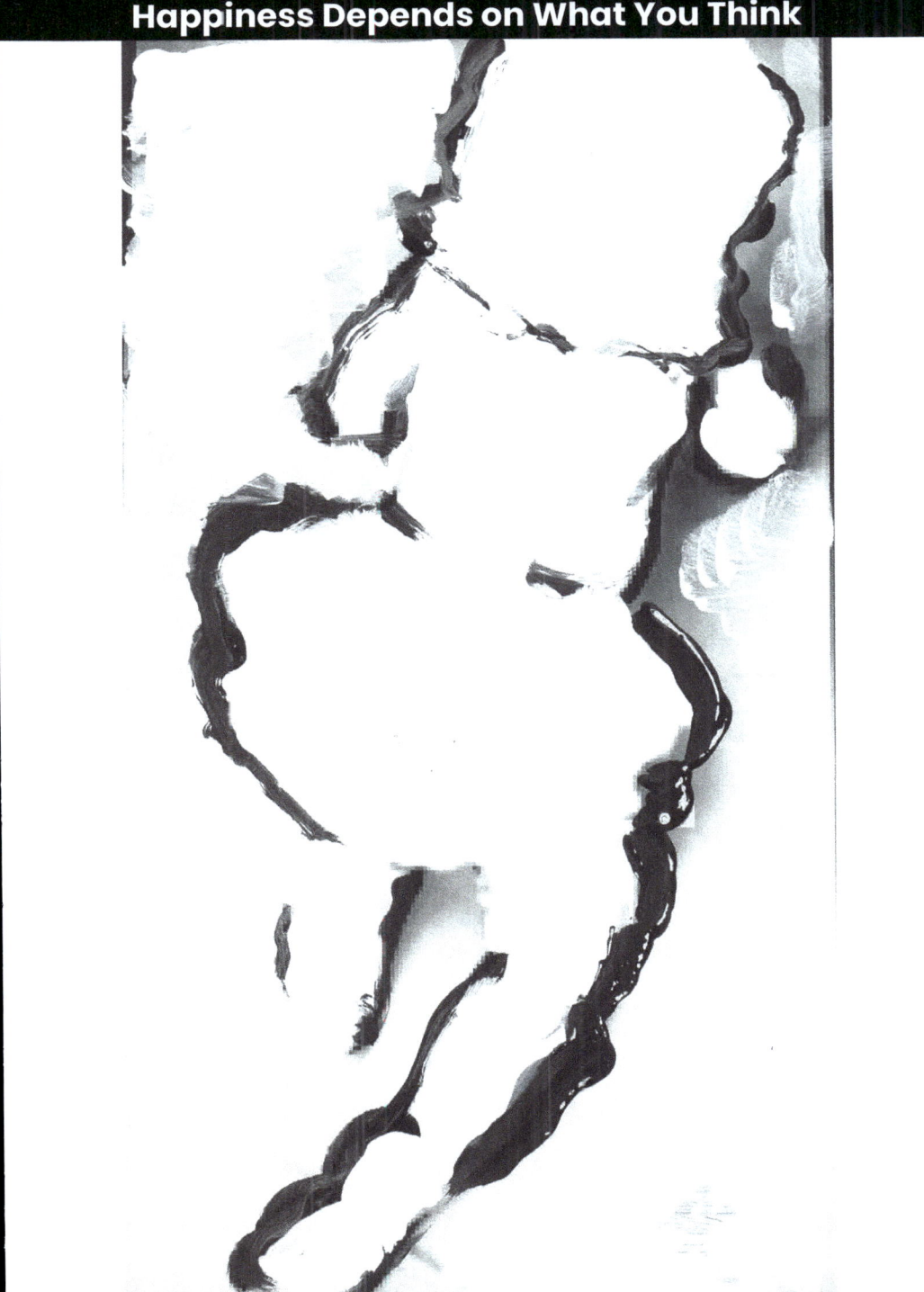

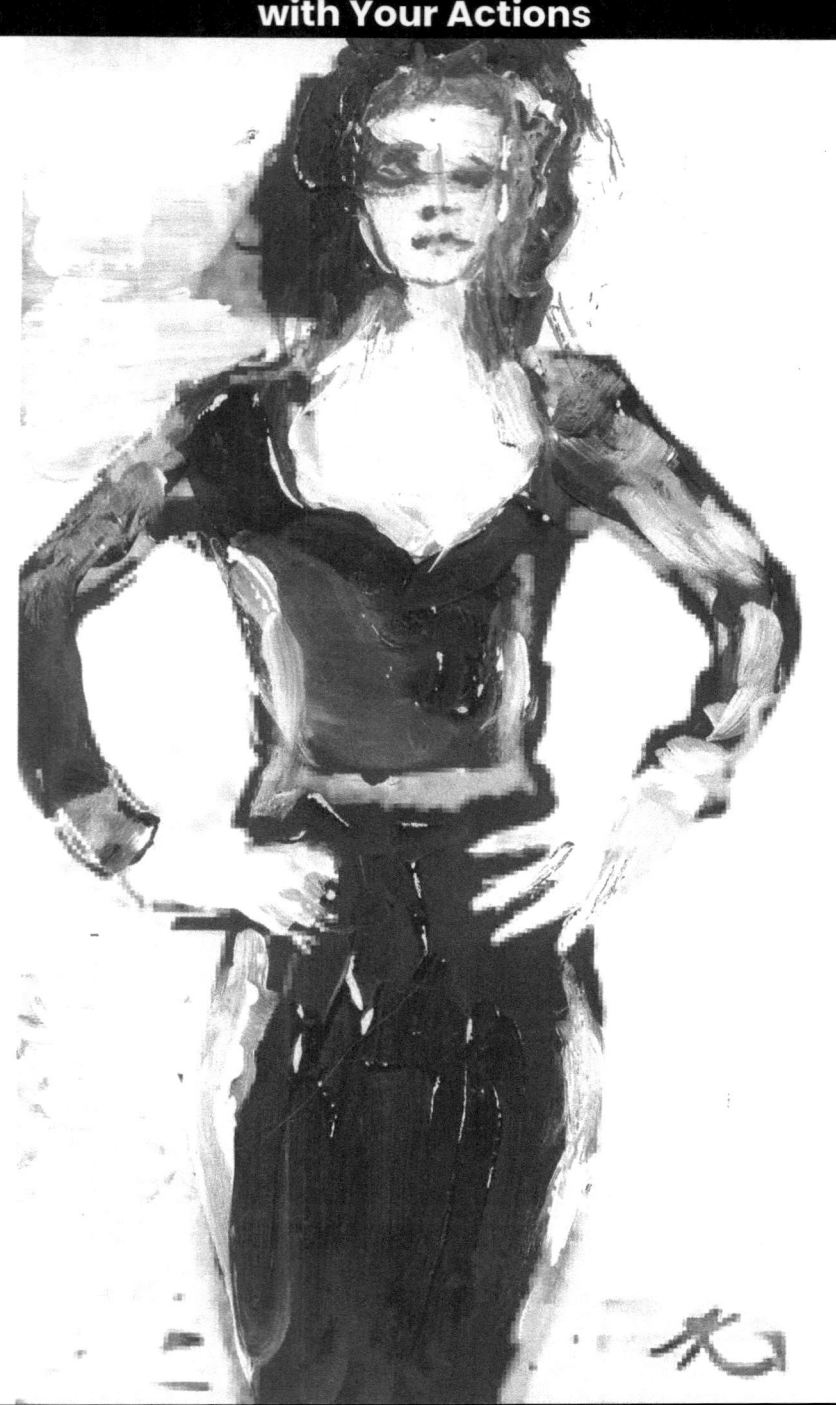

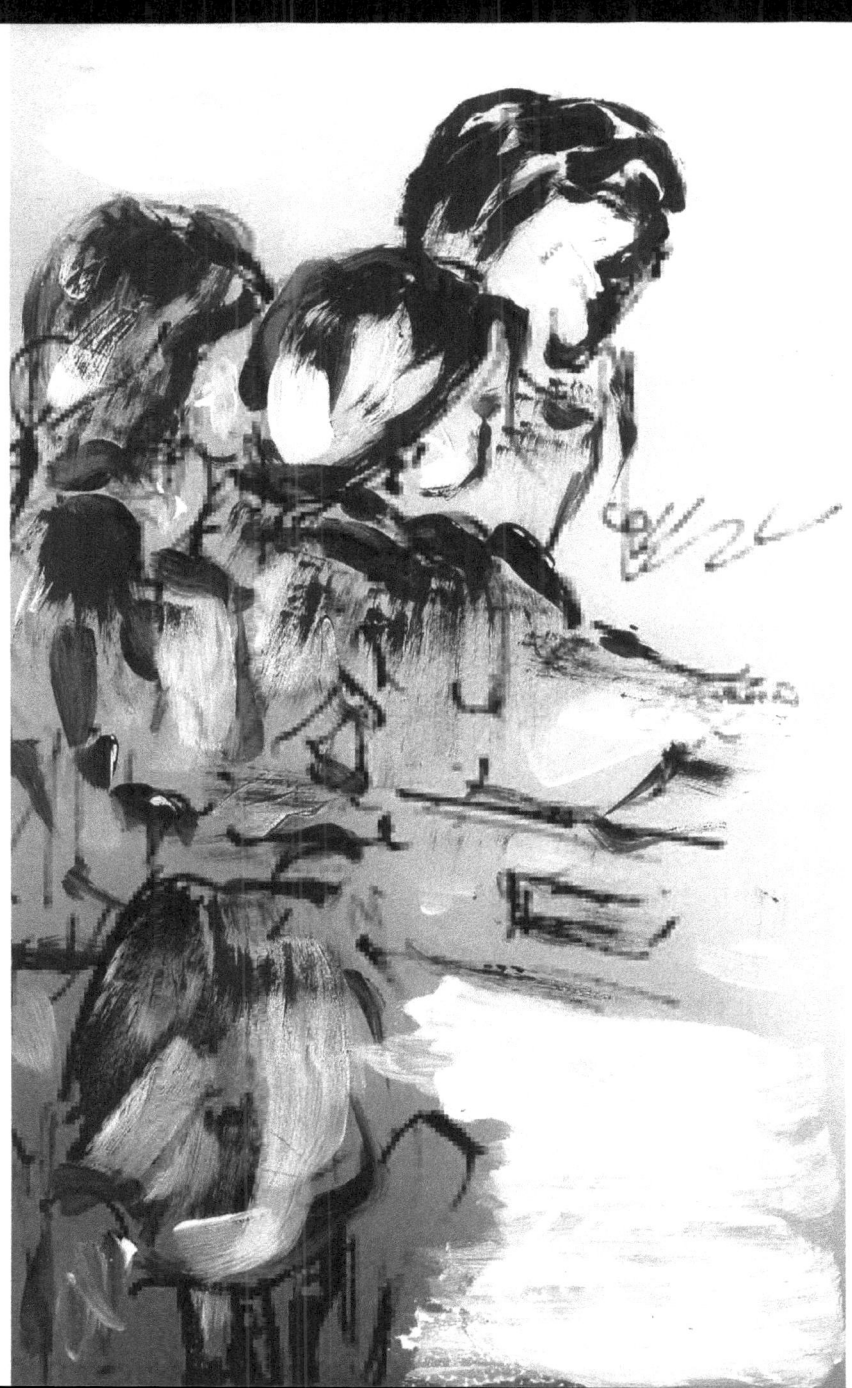

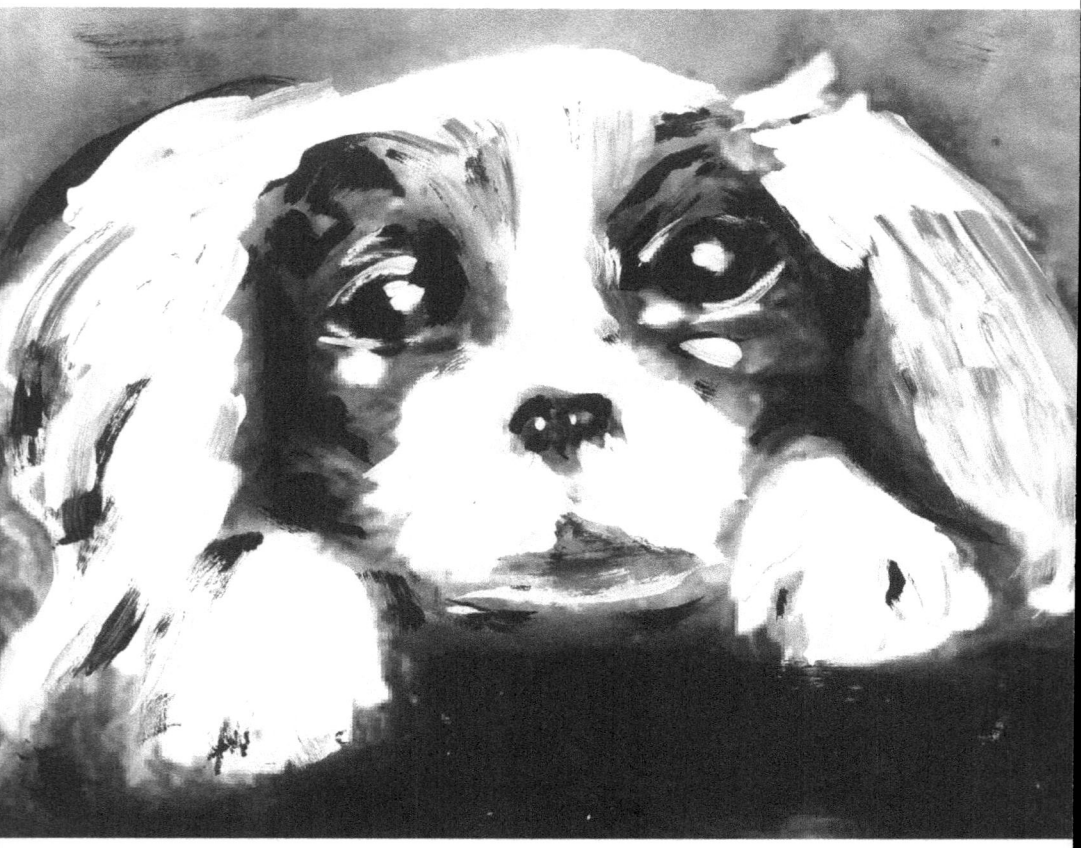

Be Happy. We are not Here Forever

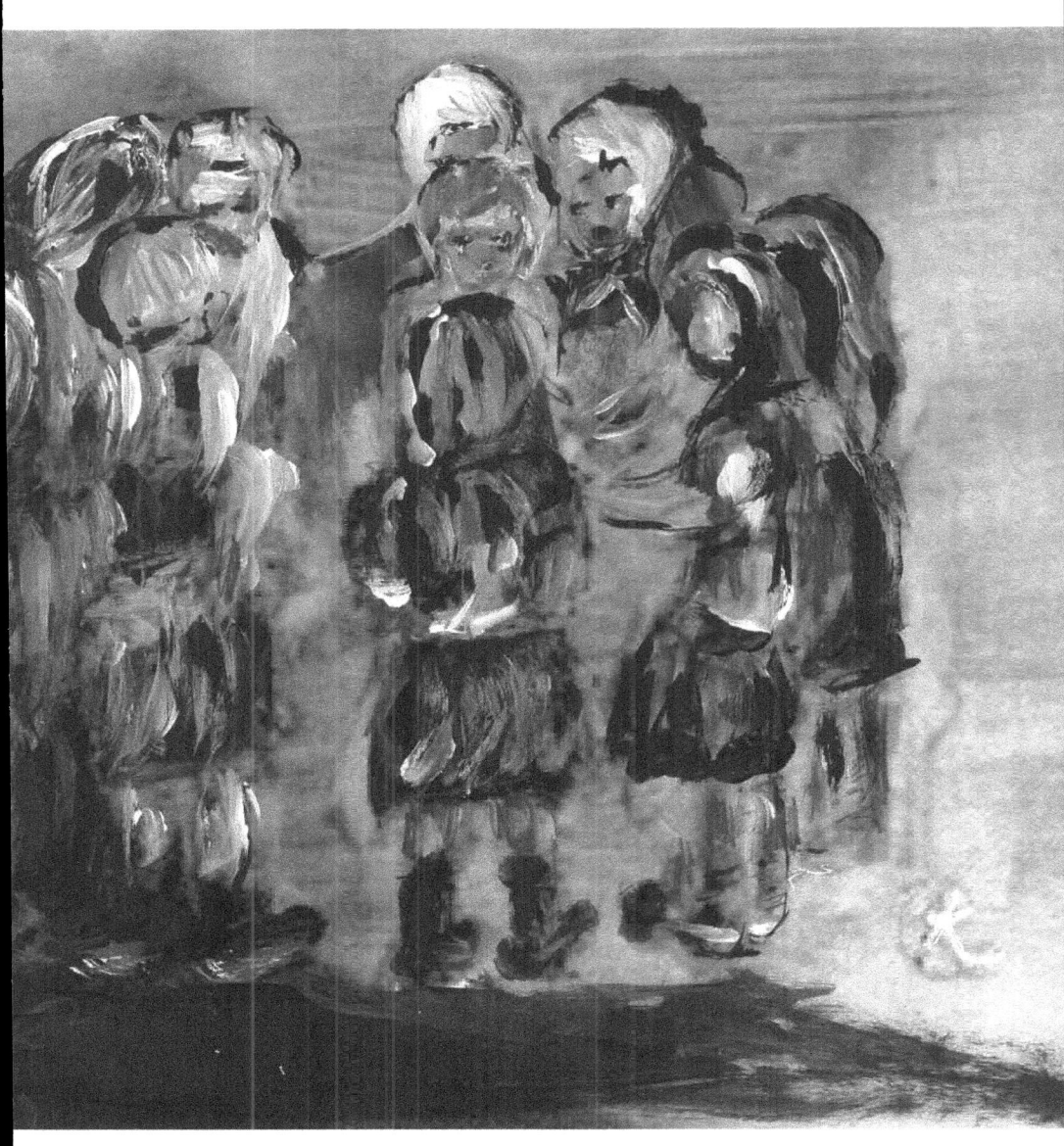

I am not this Hair. I am not this Skin. I am the Soul that Lives Within

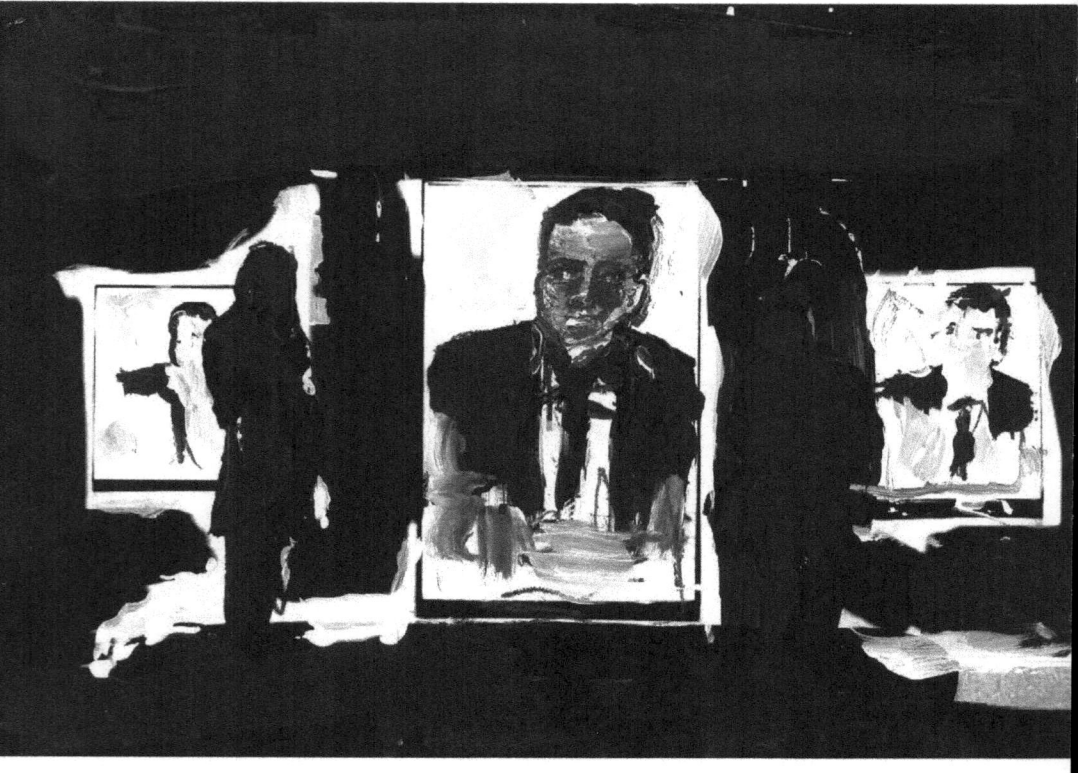

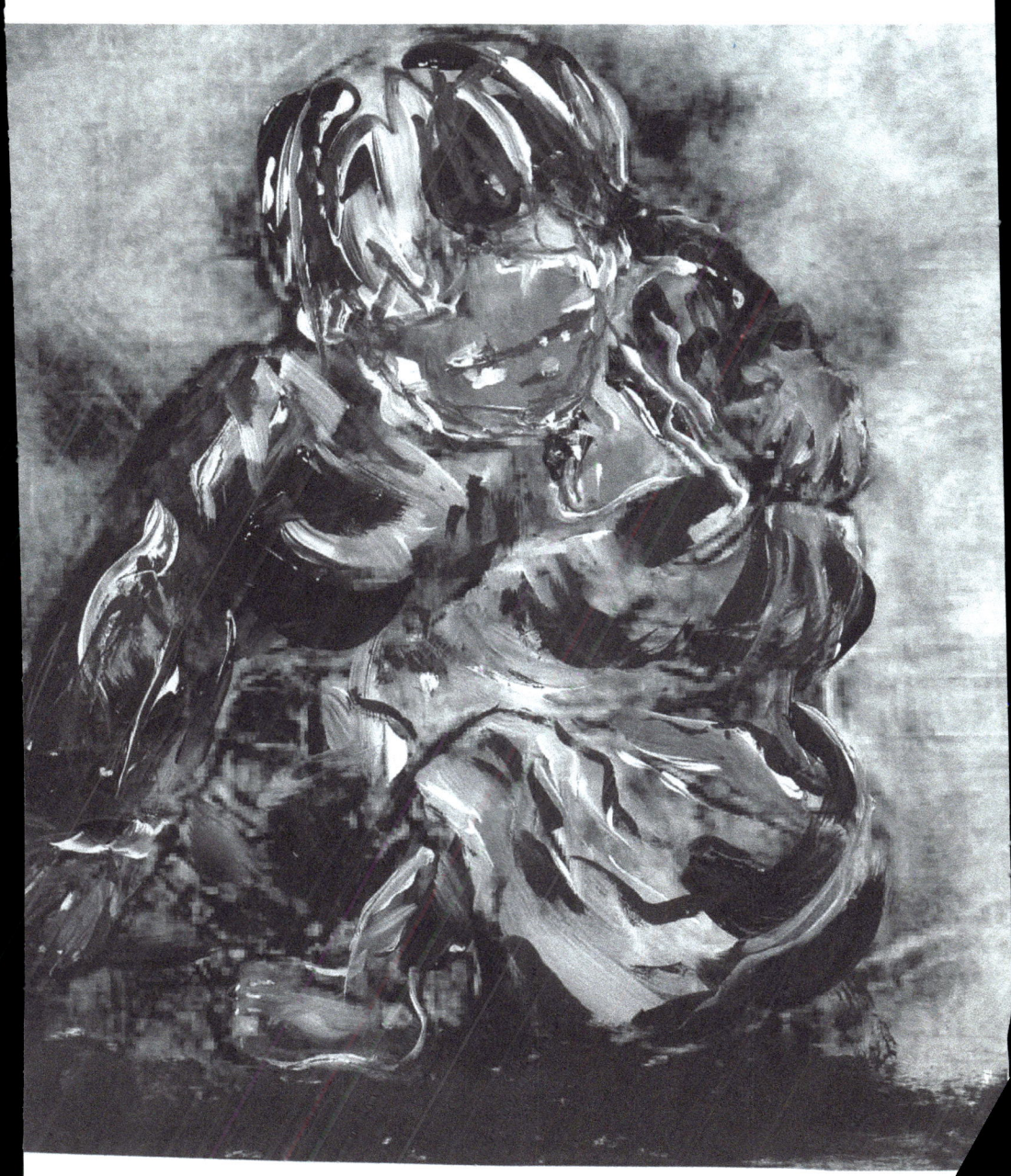

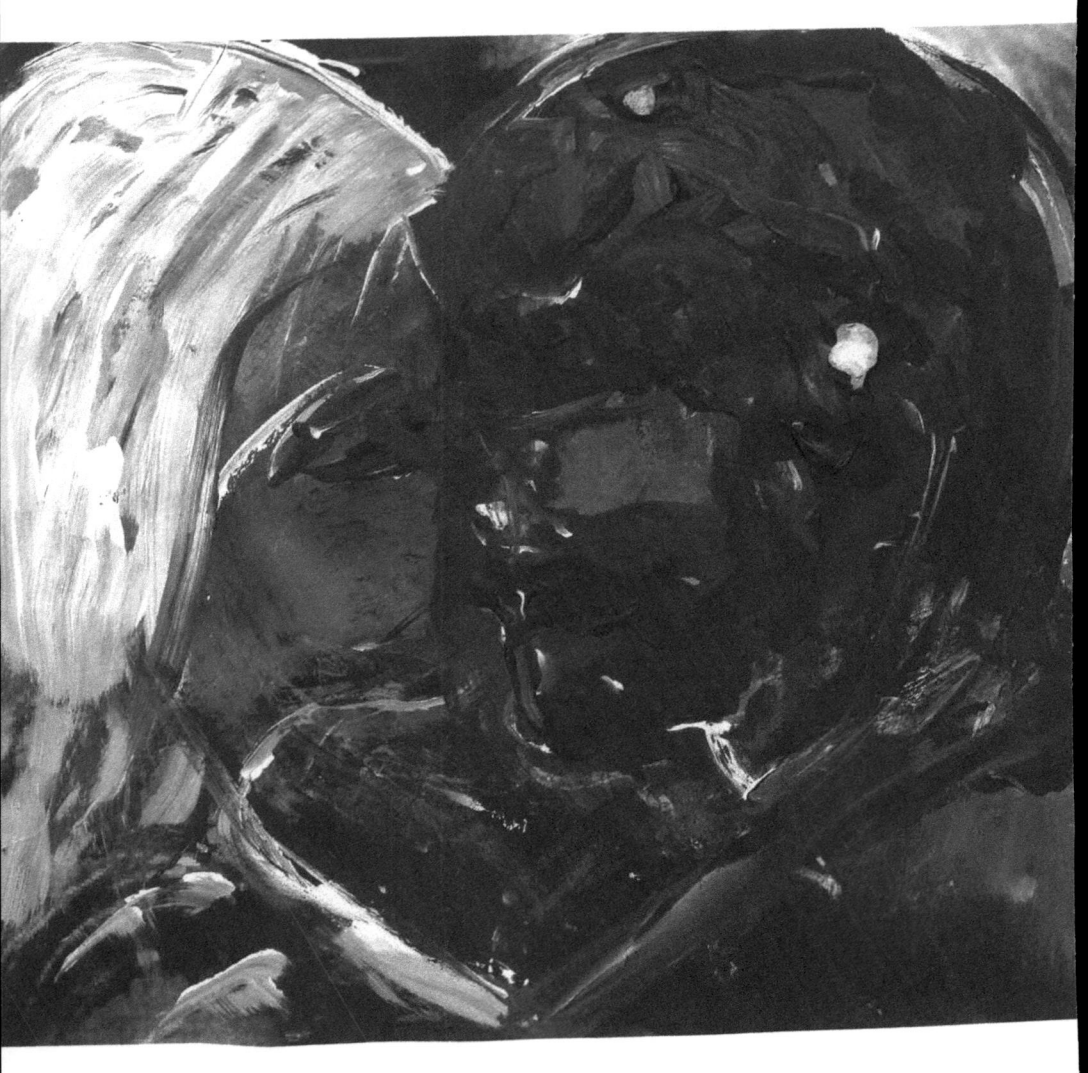

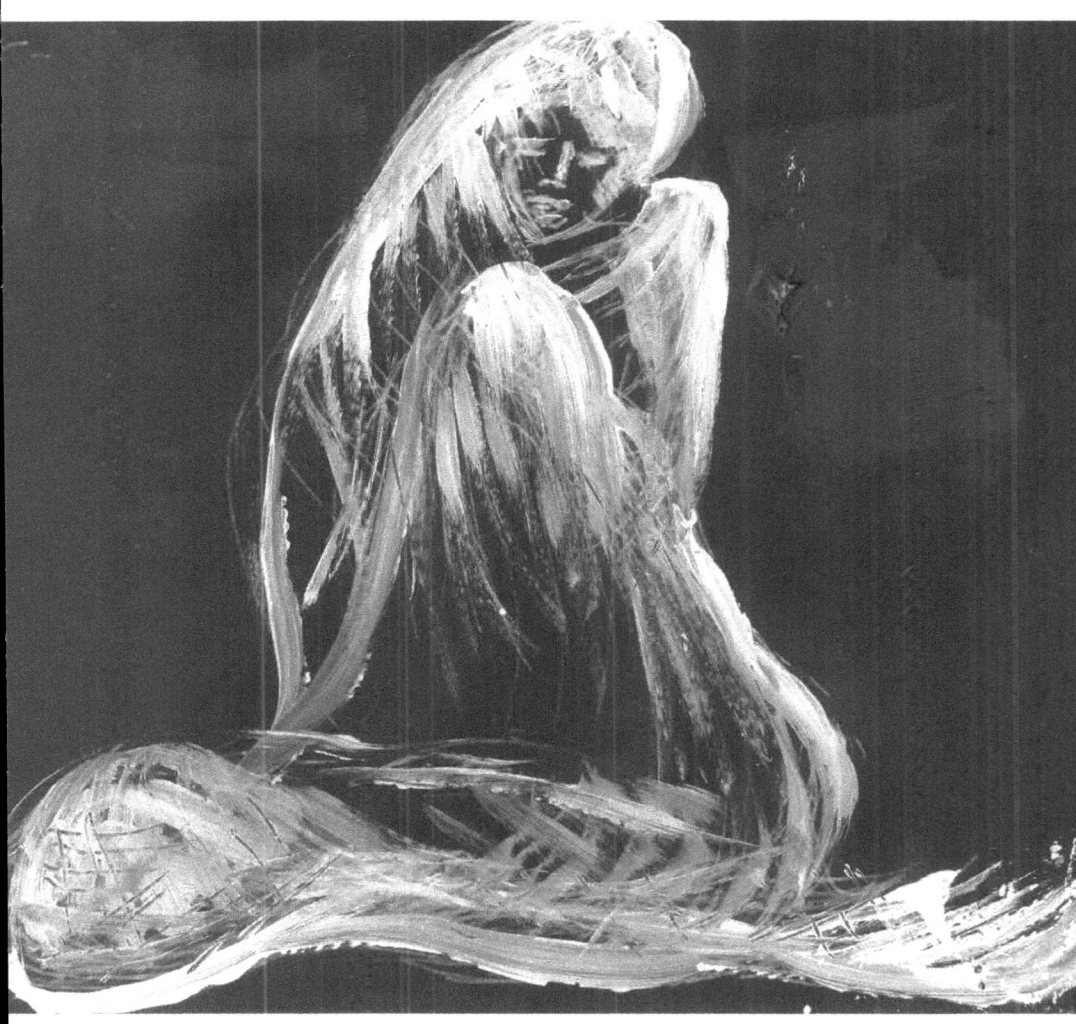

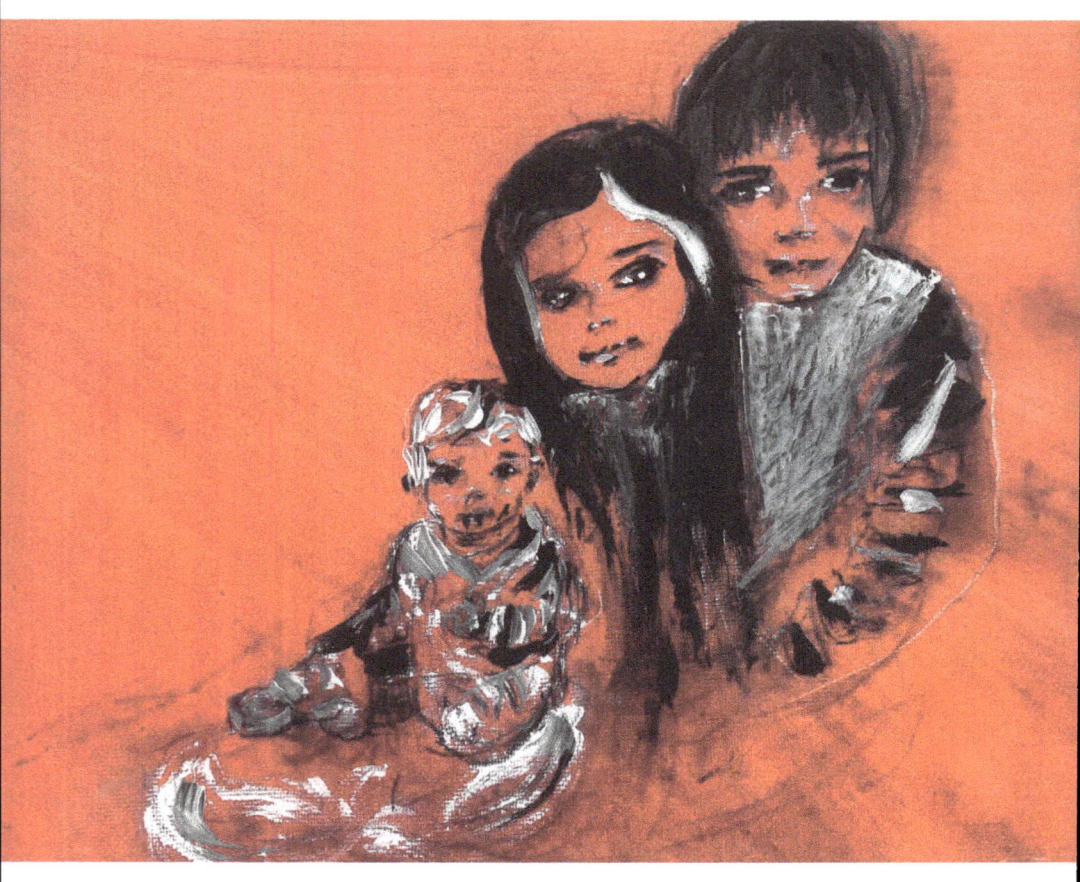

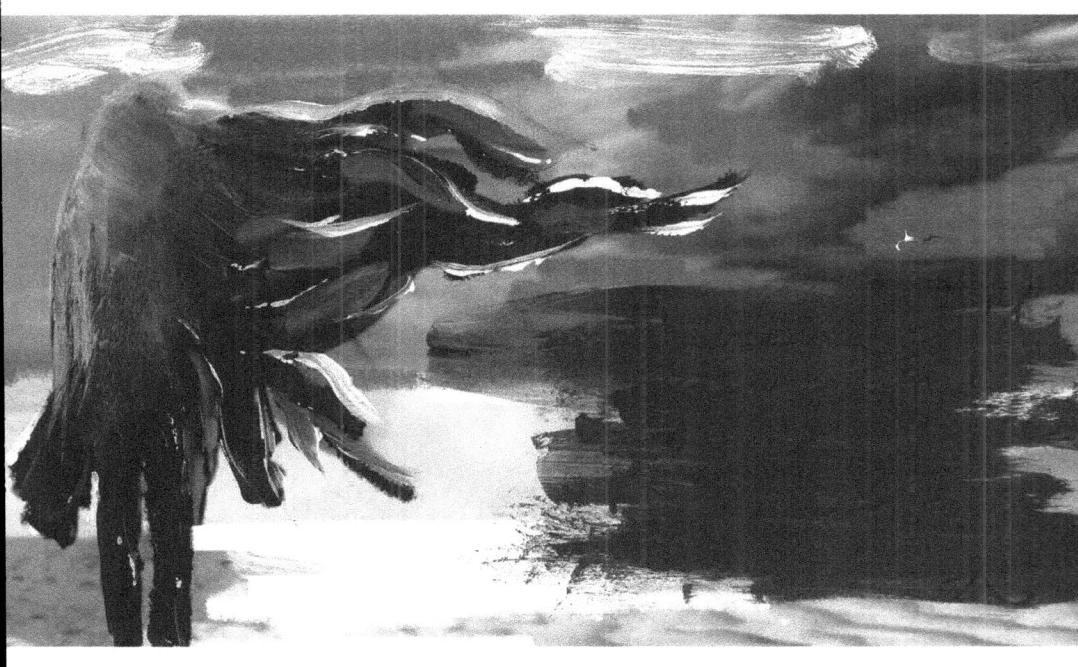

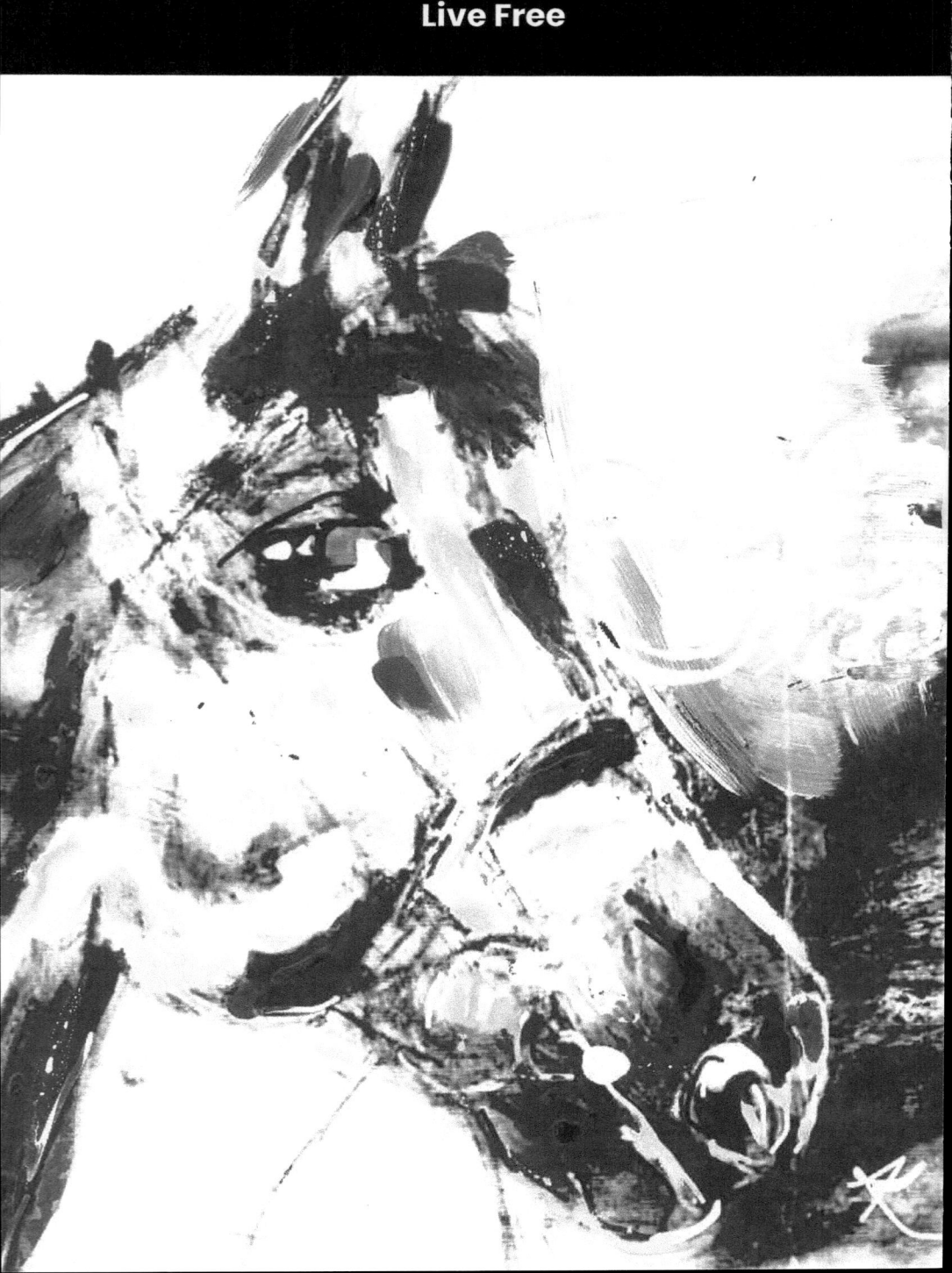

When Something is Gone, Something Better is Coming

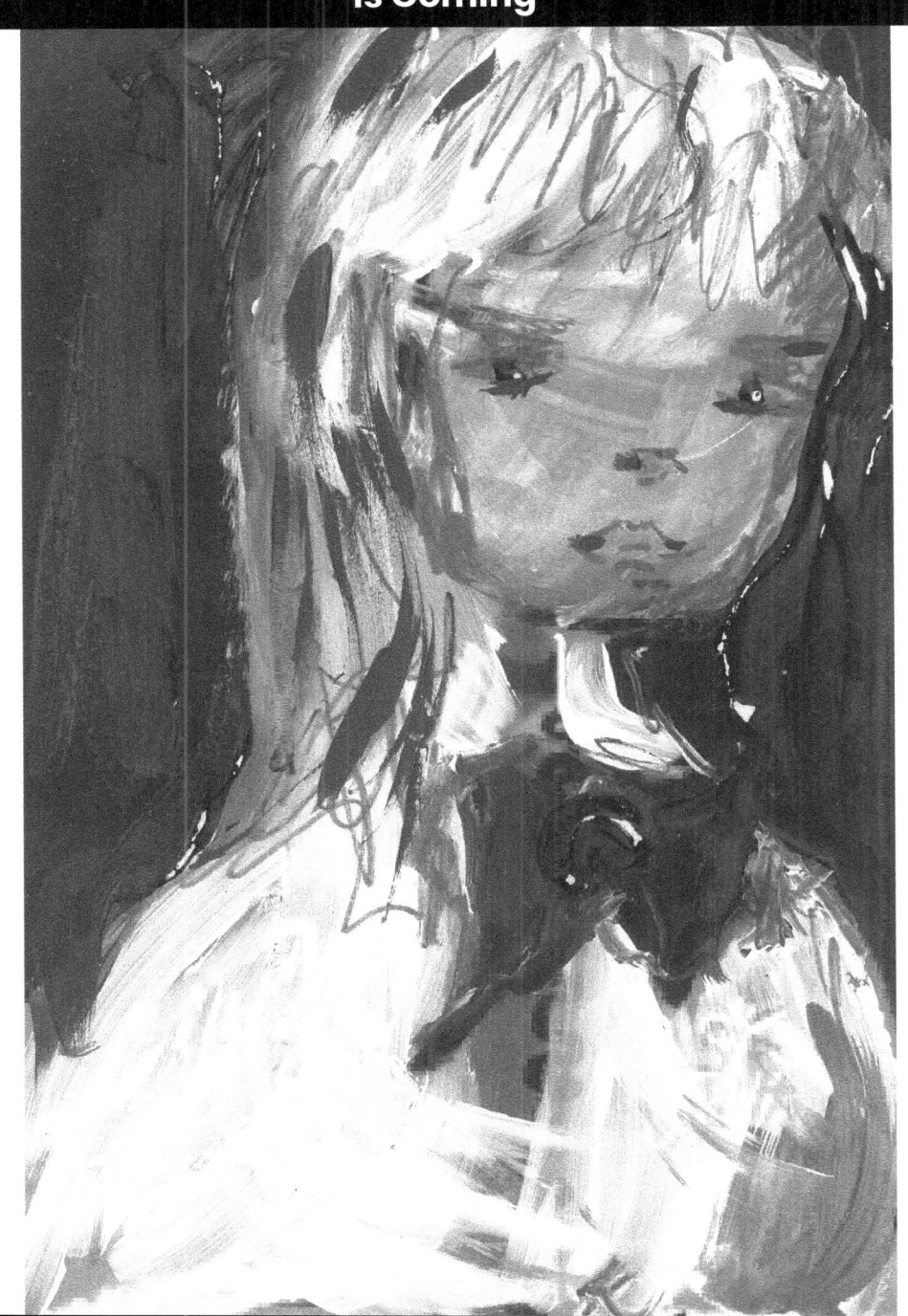

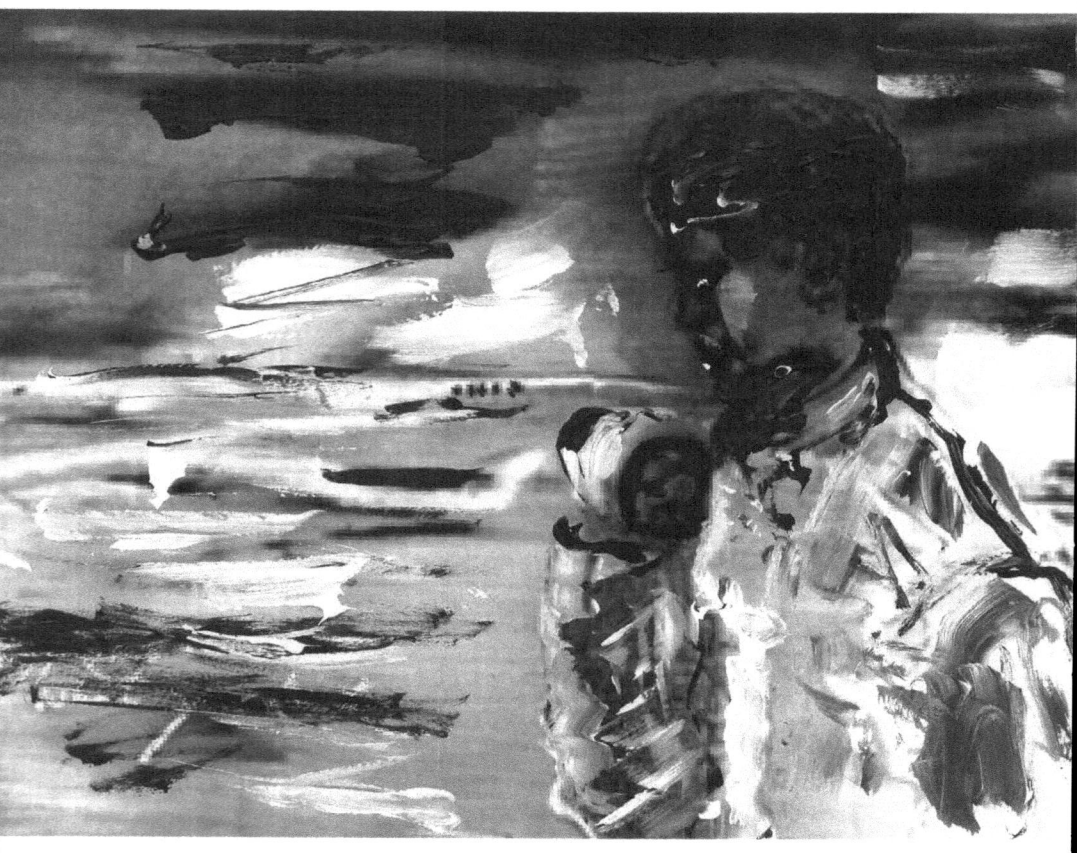

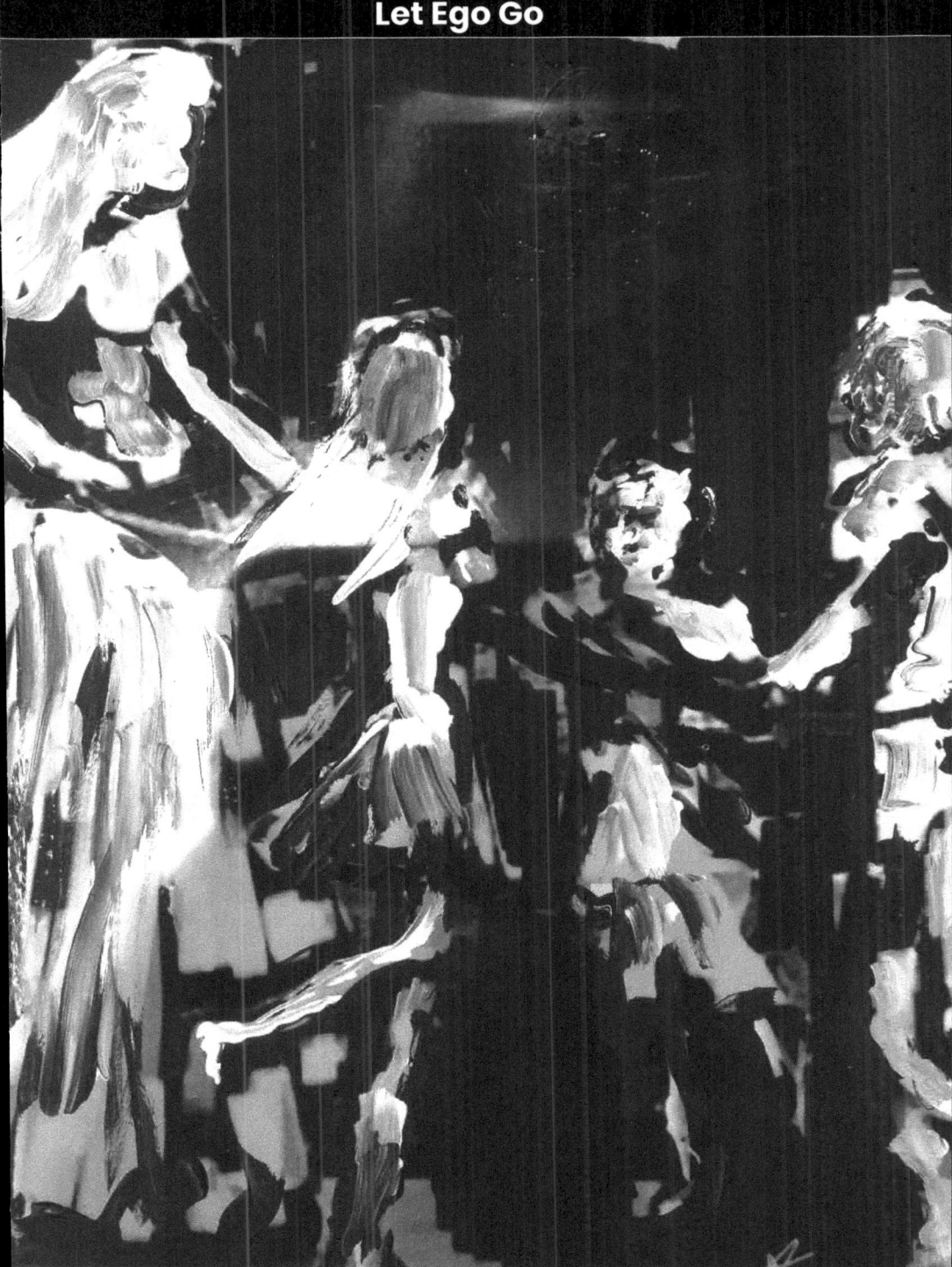

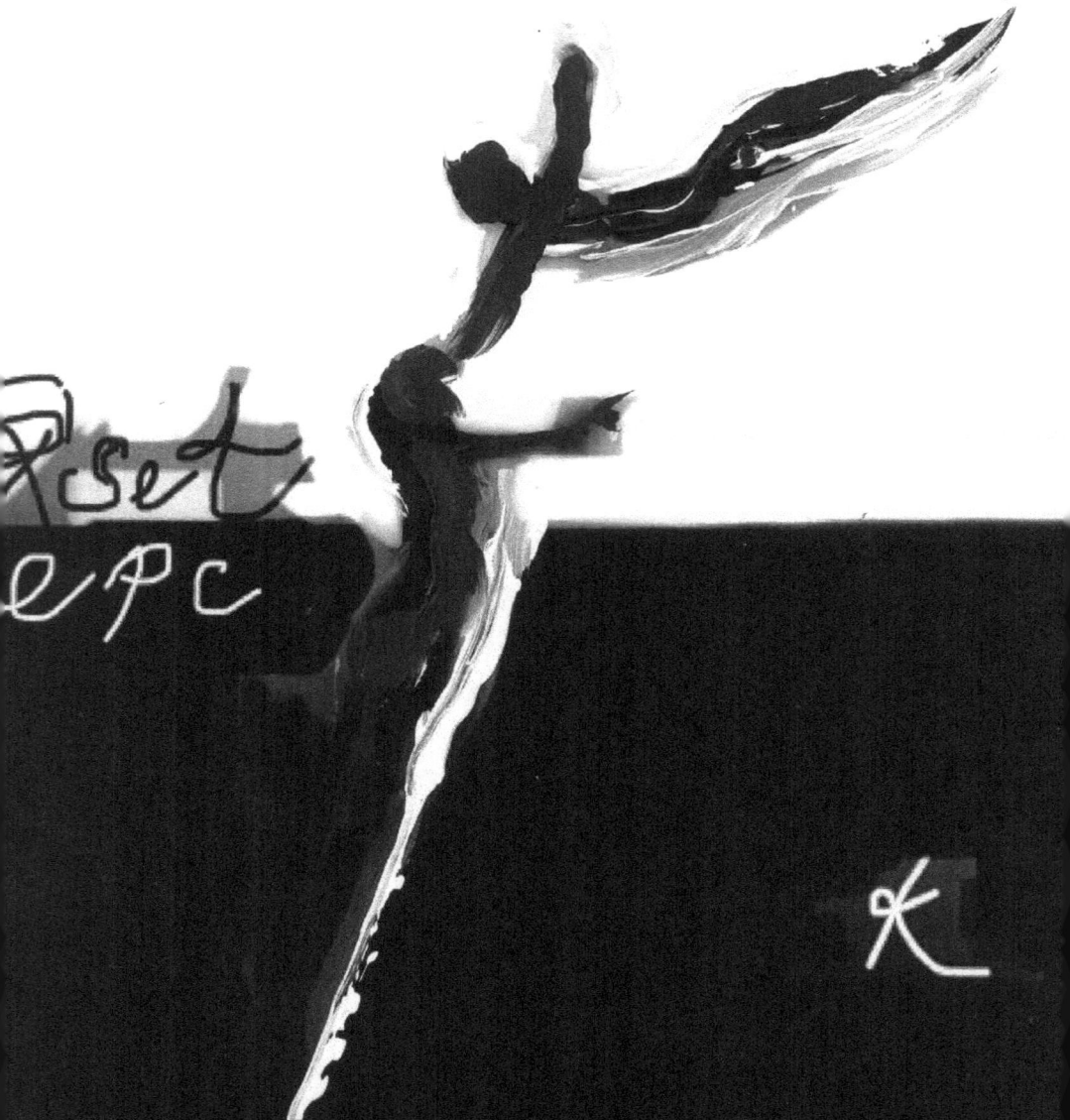

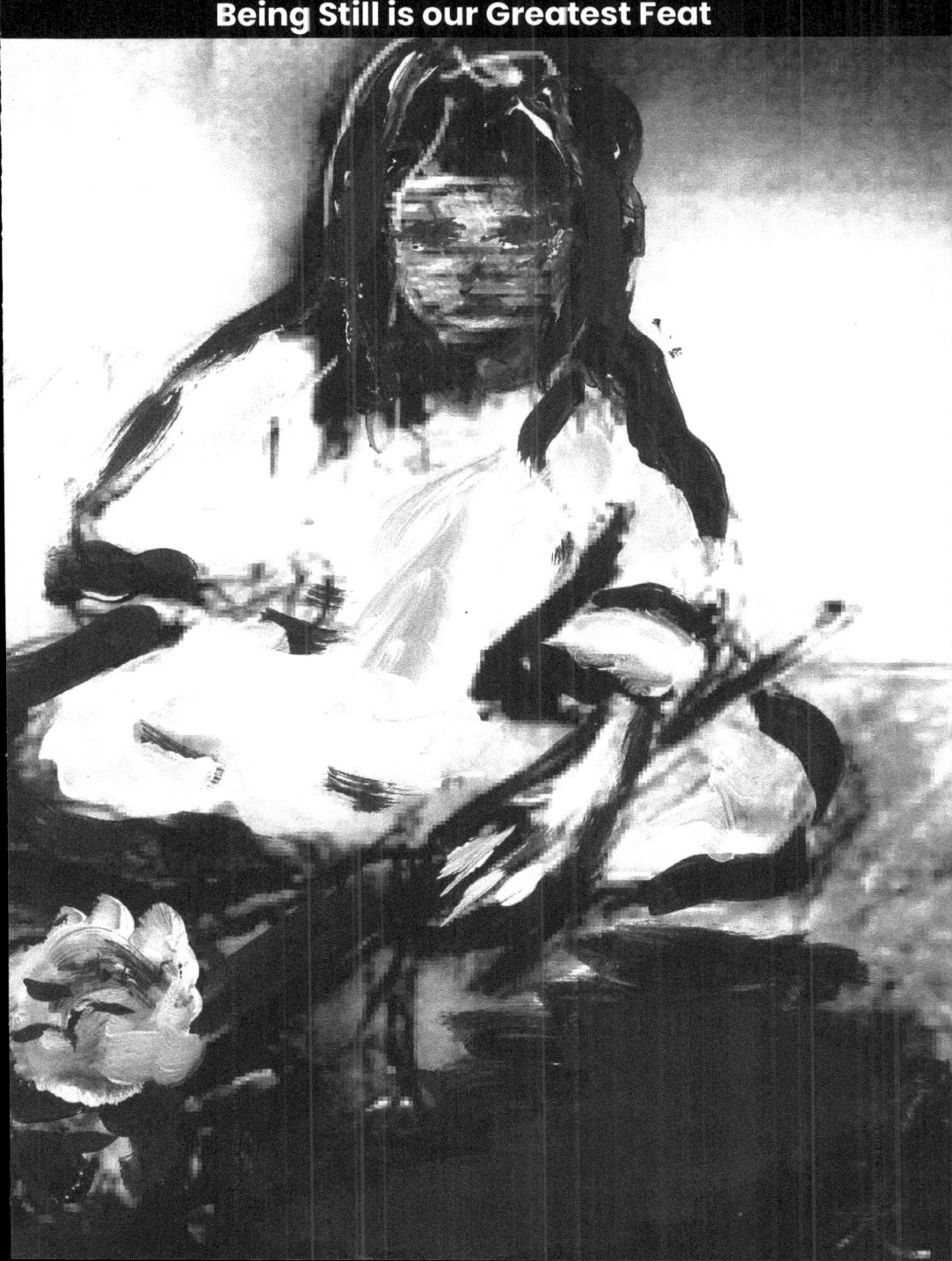
Being Still is our Greatest Feat

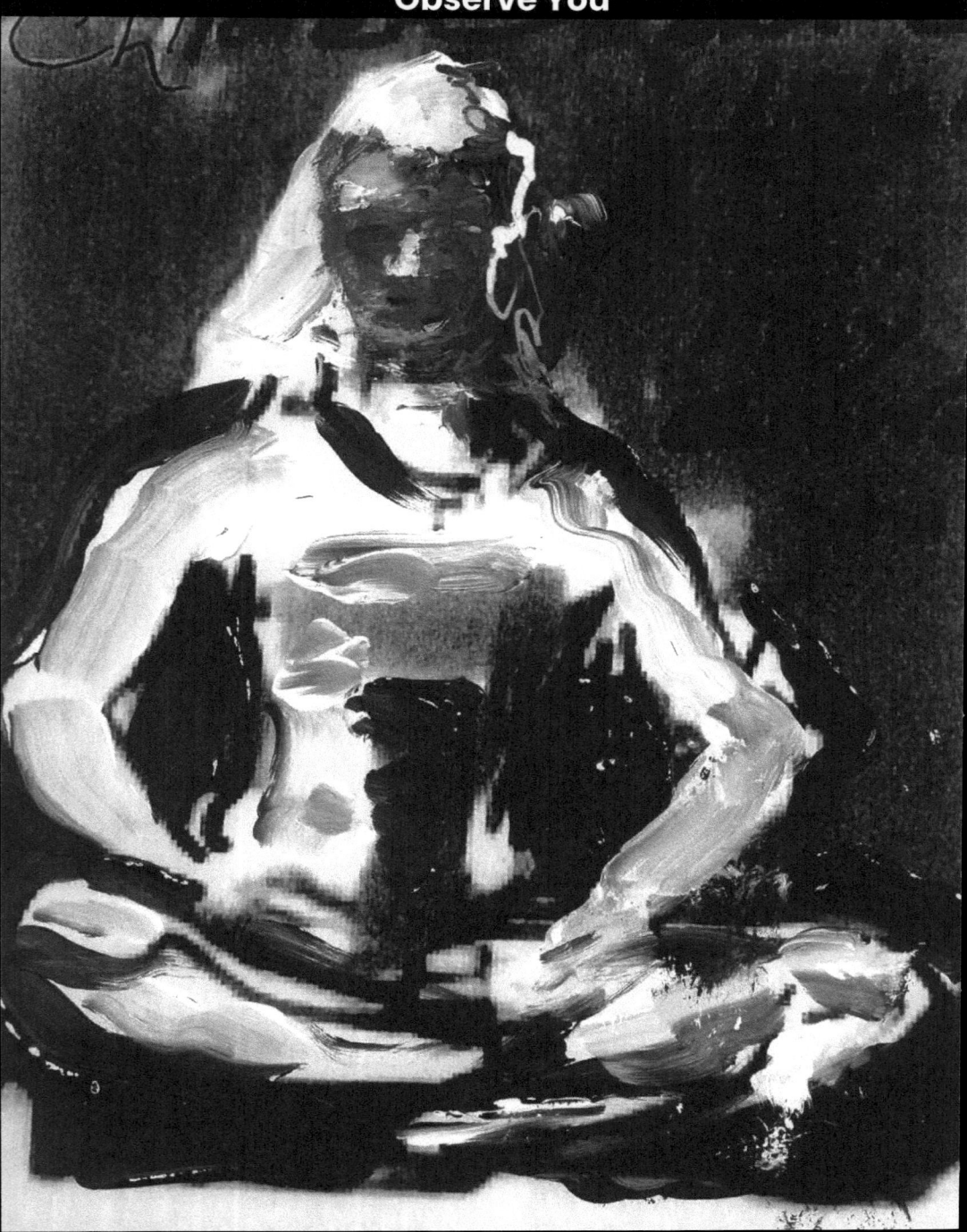

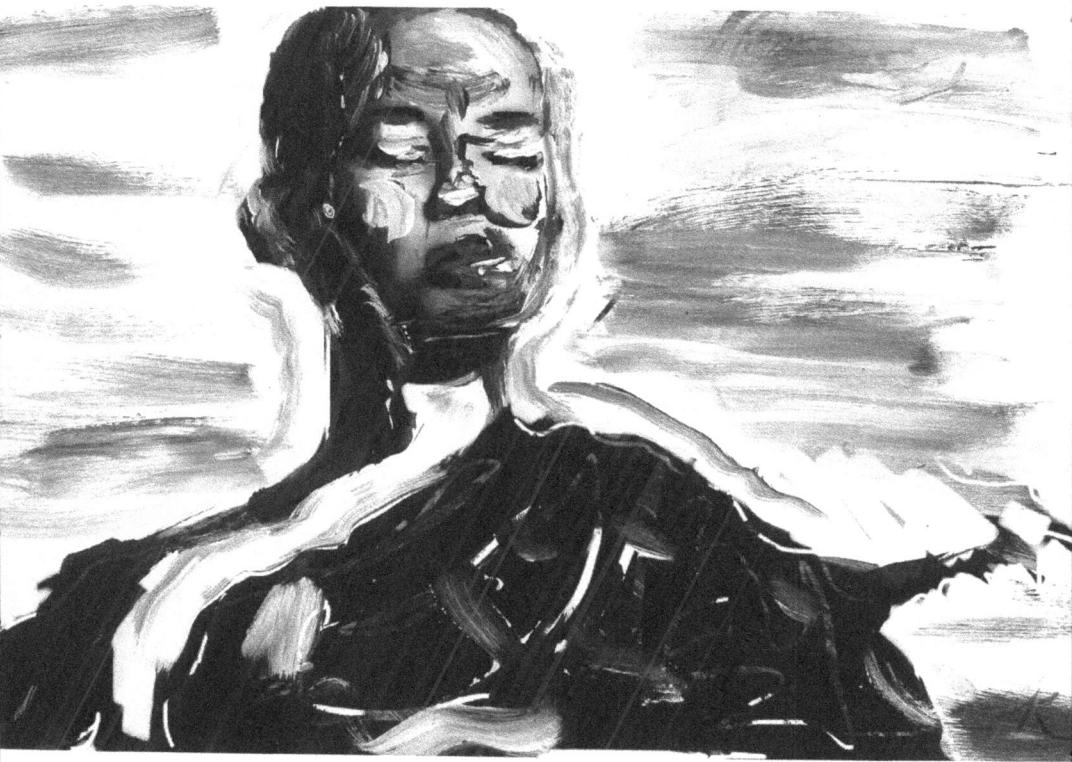

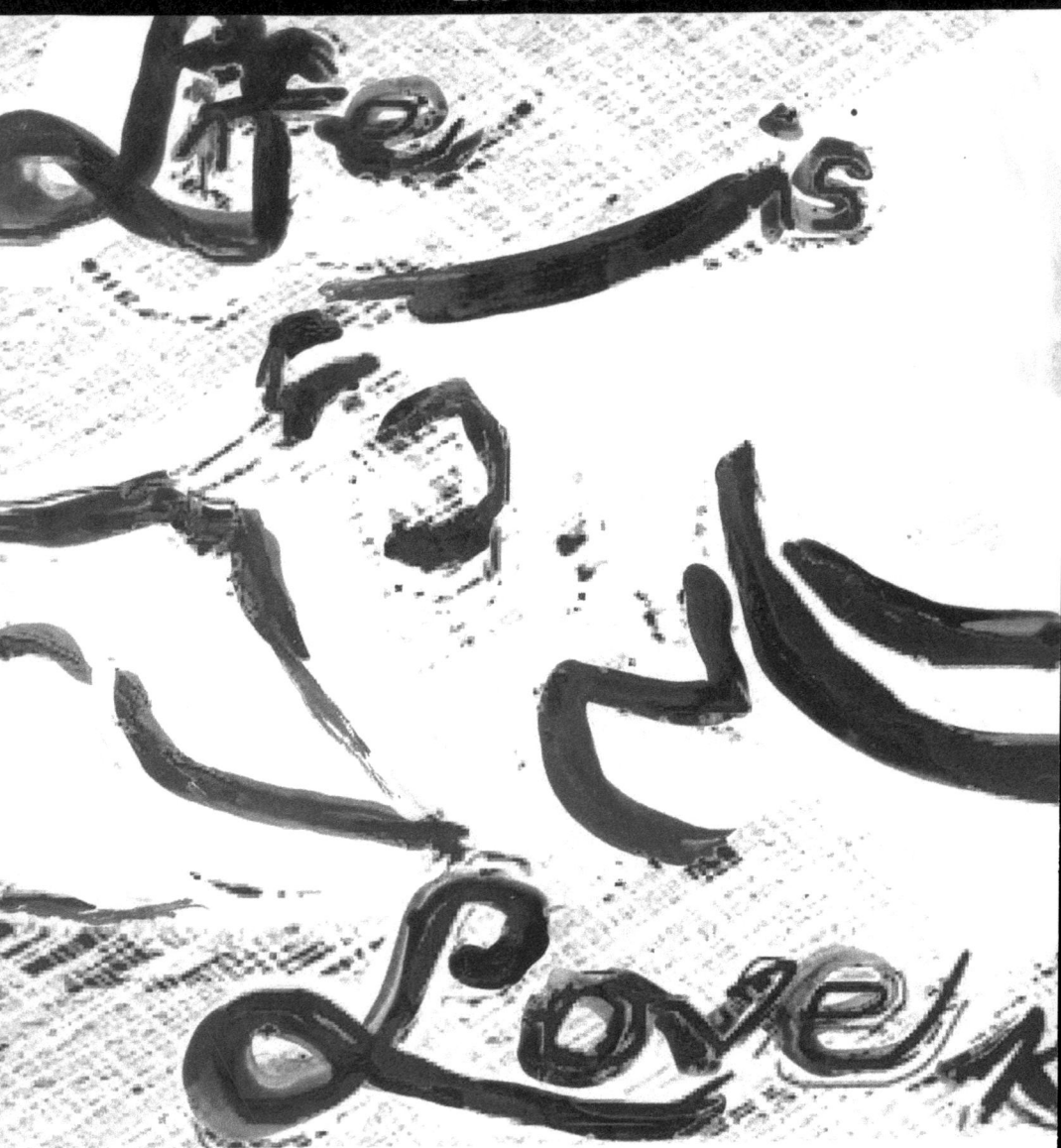

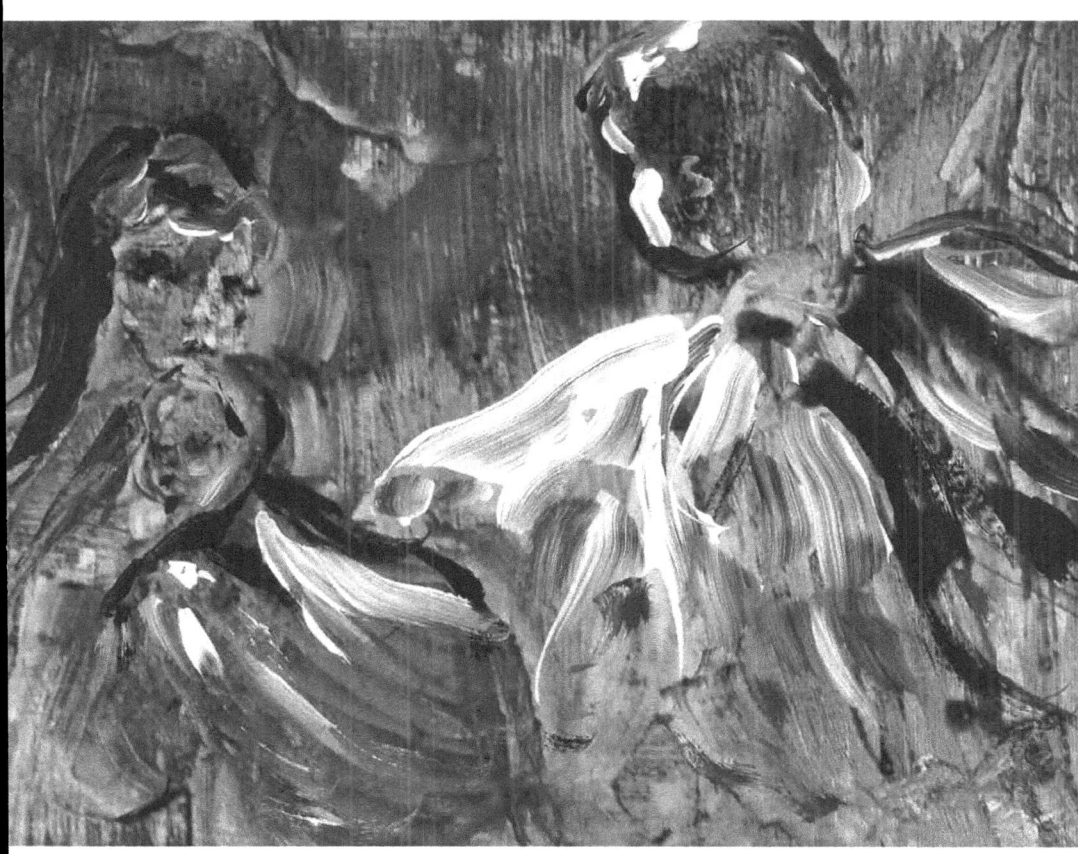

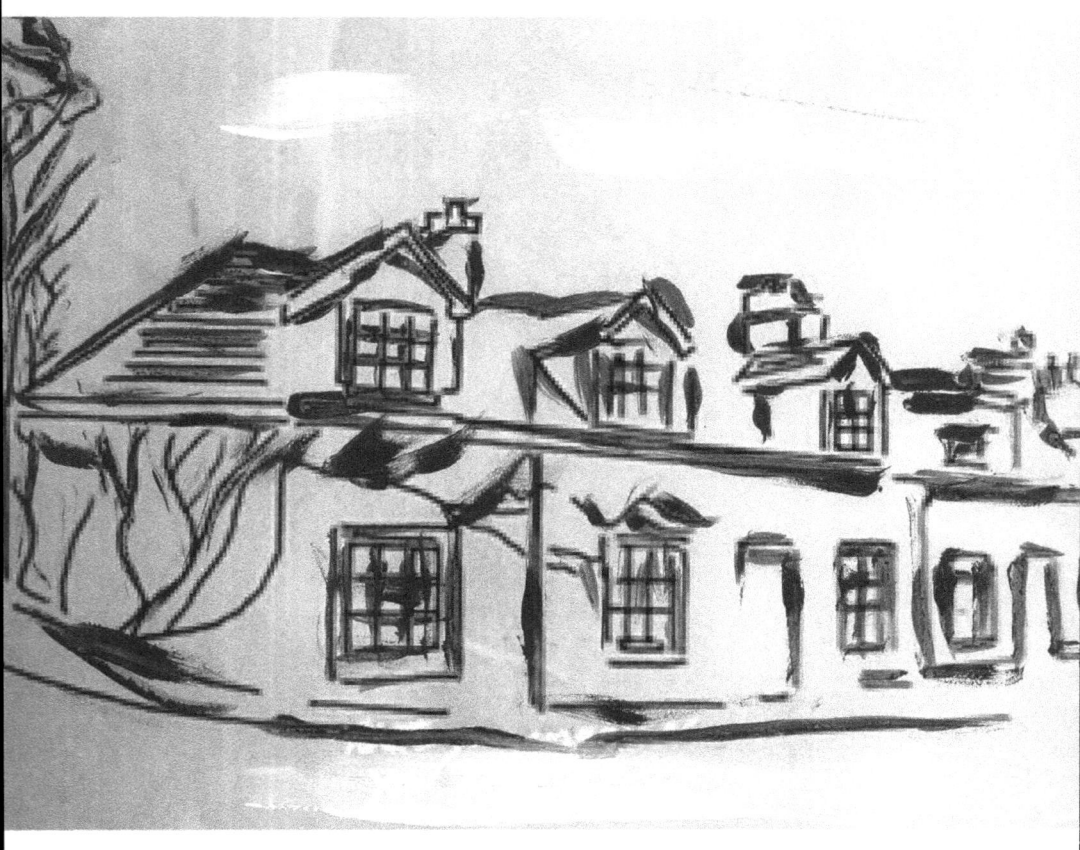

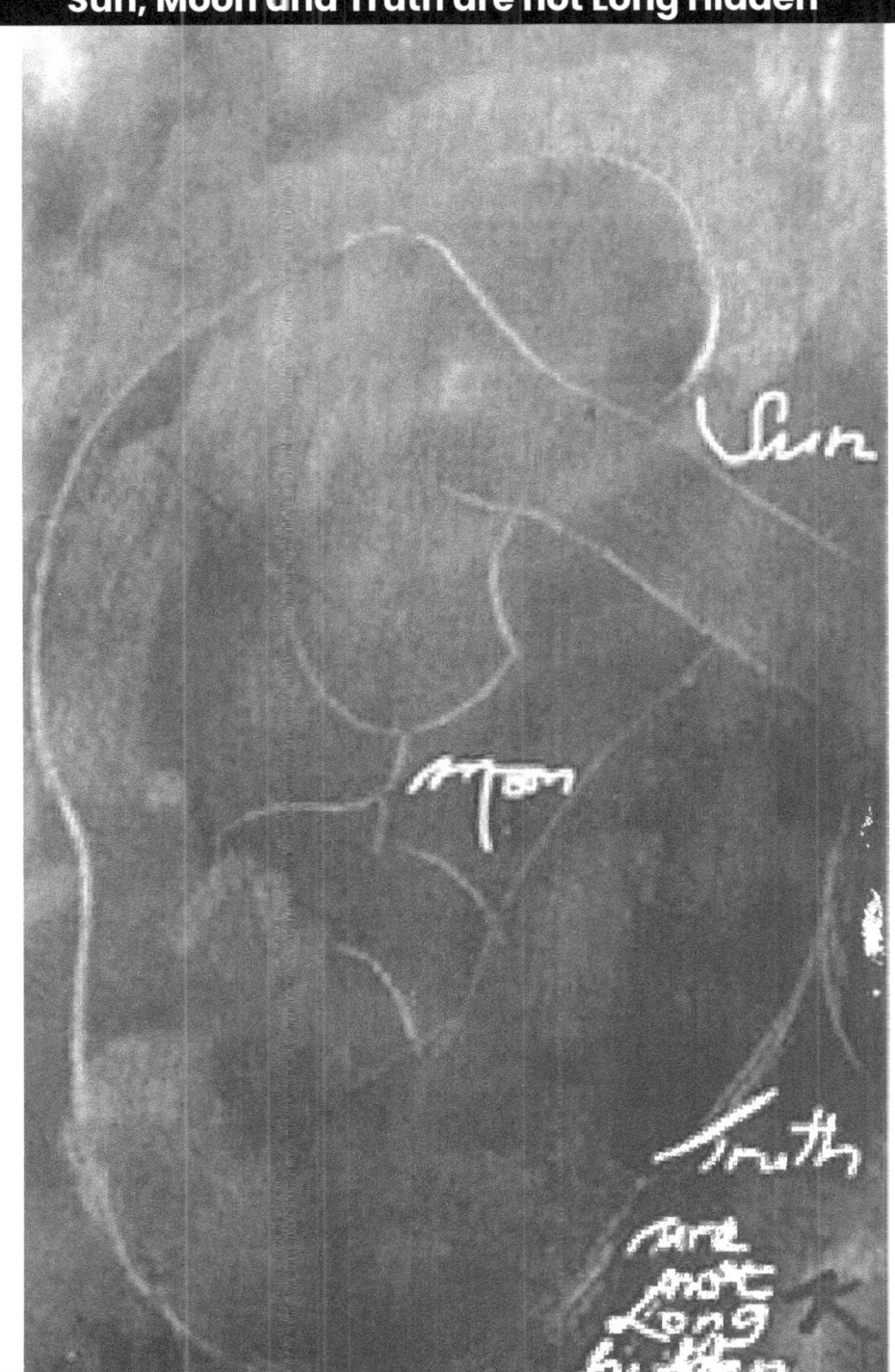

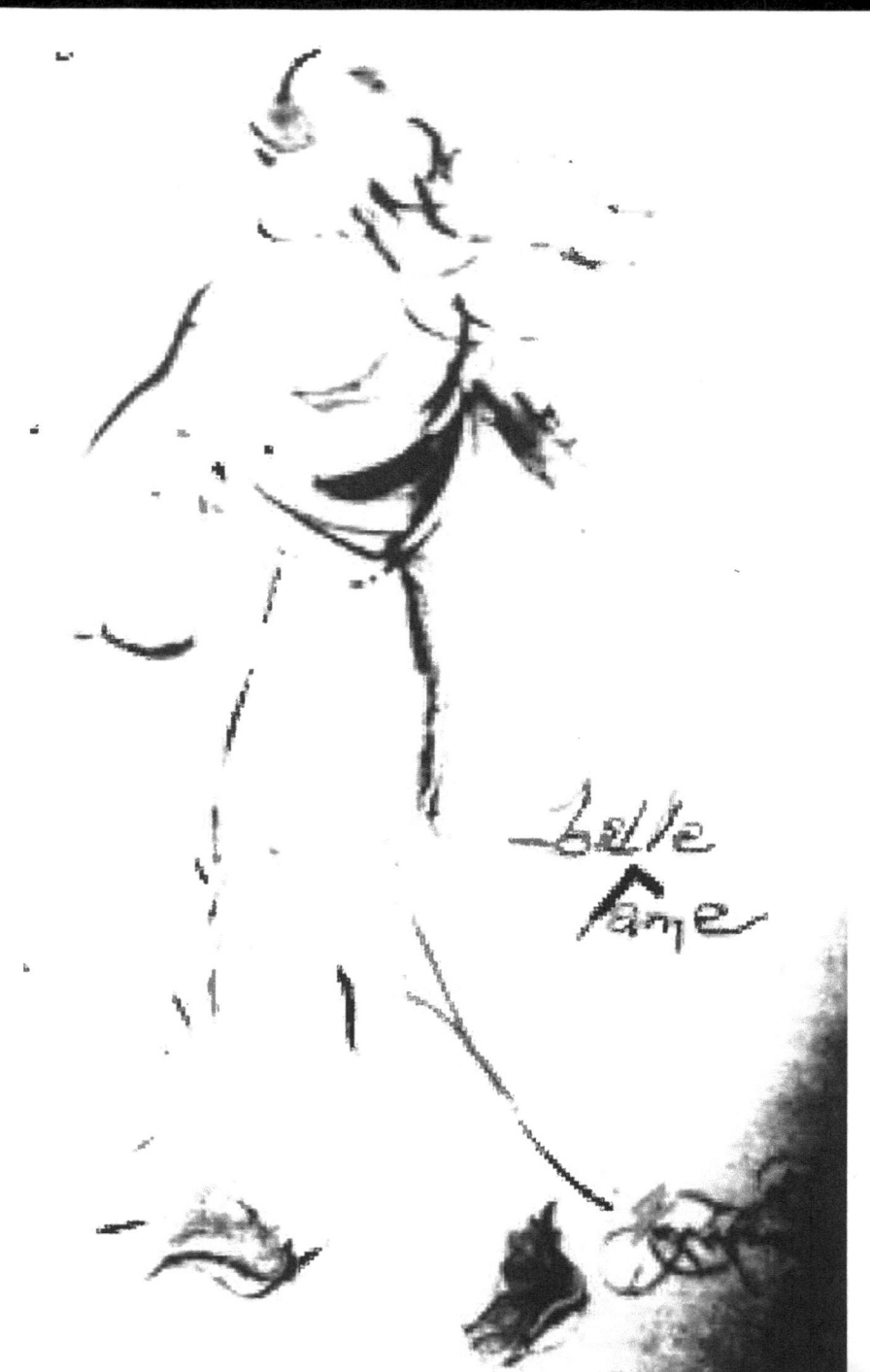

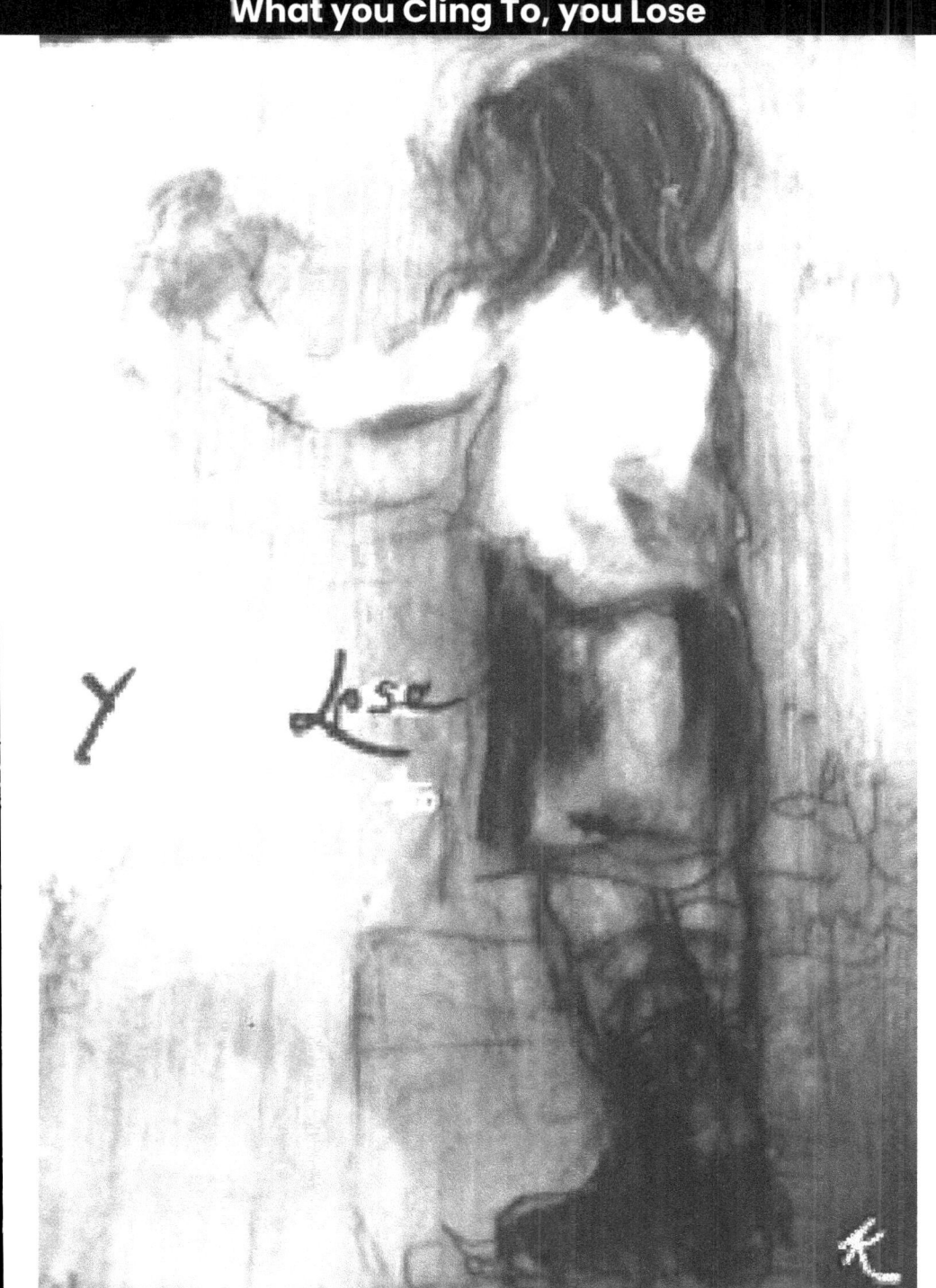

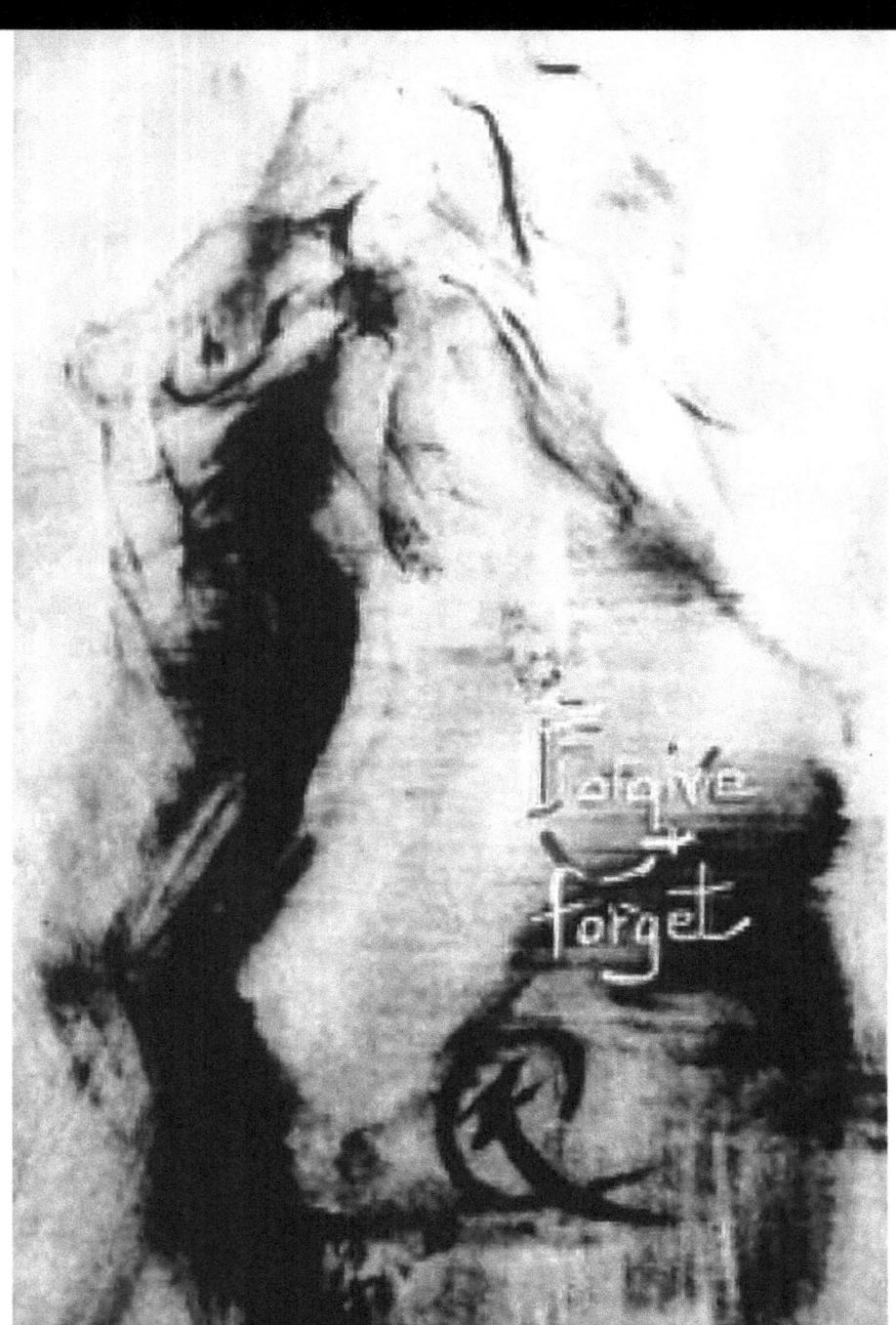

All that Matters is: How you Loved, How Gently you Lived, How Gracefully you Let Go of Things not Meant for You

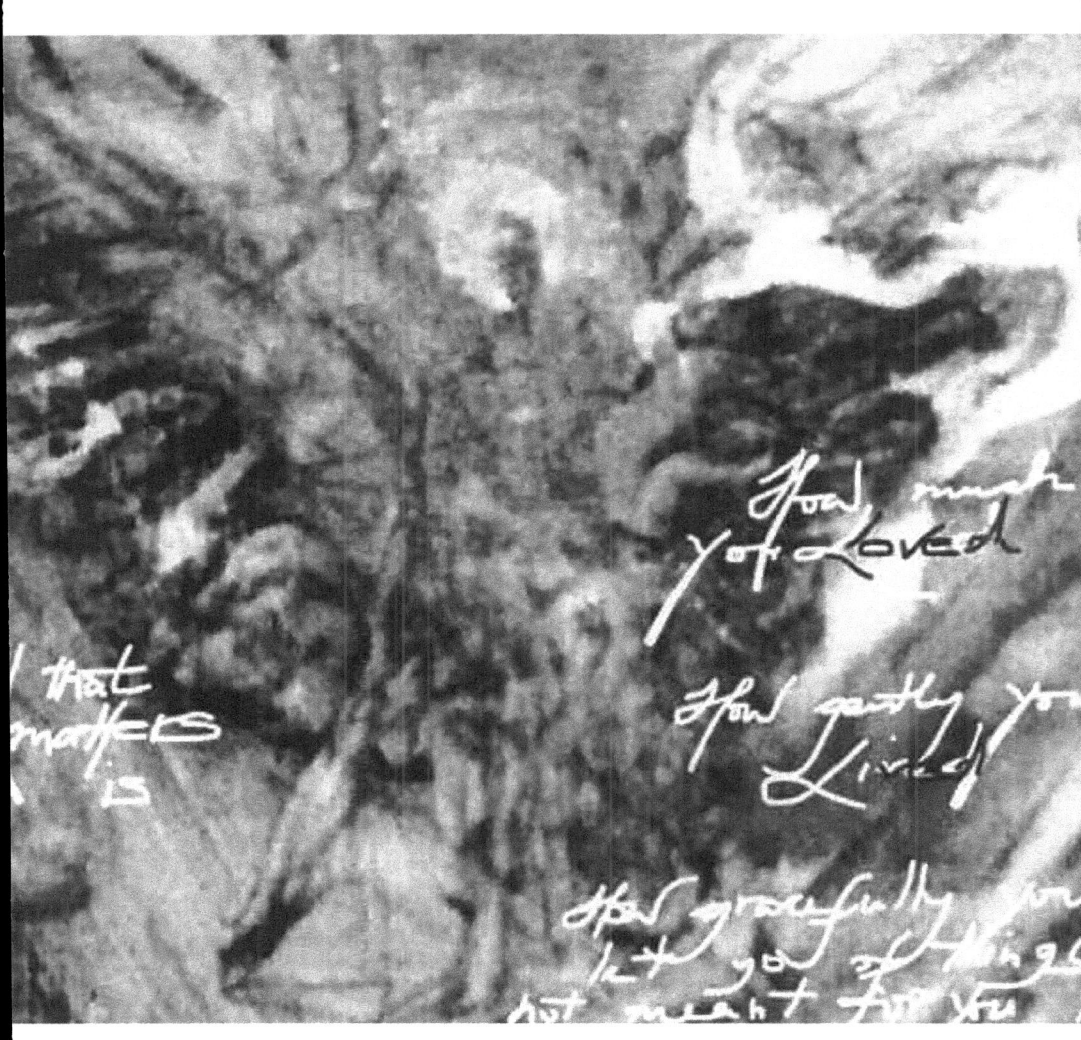

Your Mind is Powerful. Stay Positive

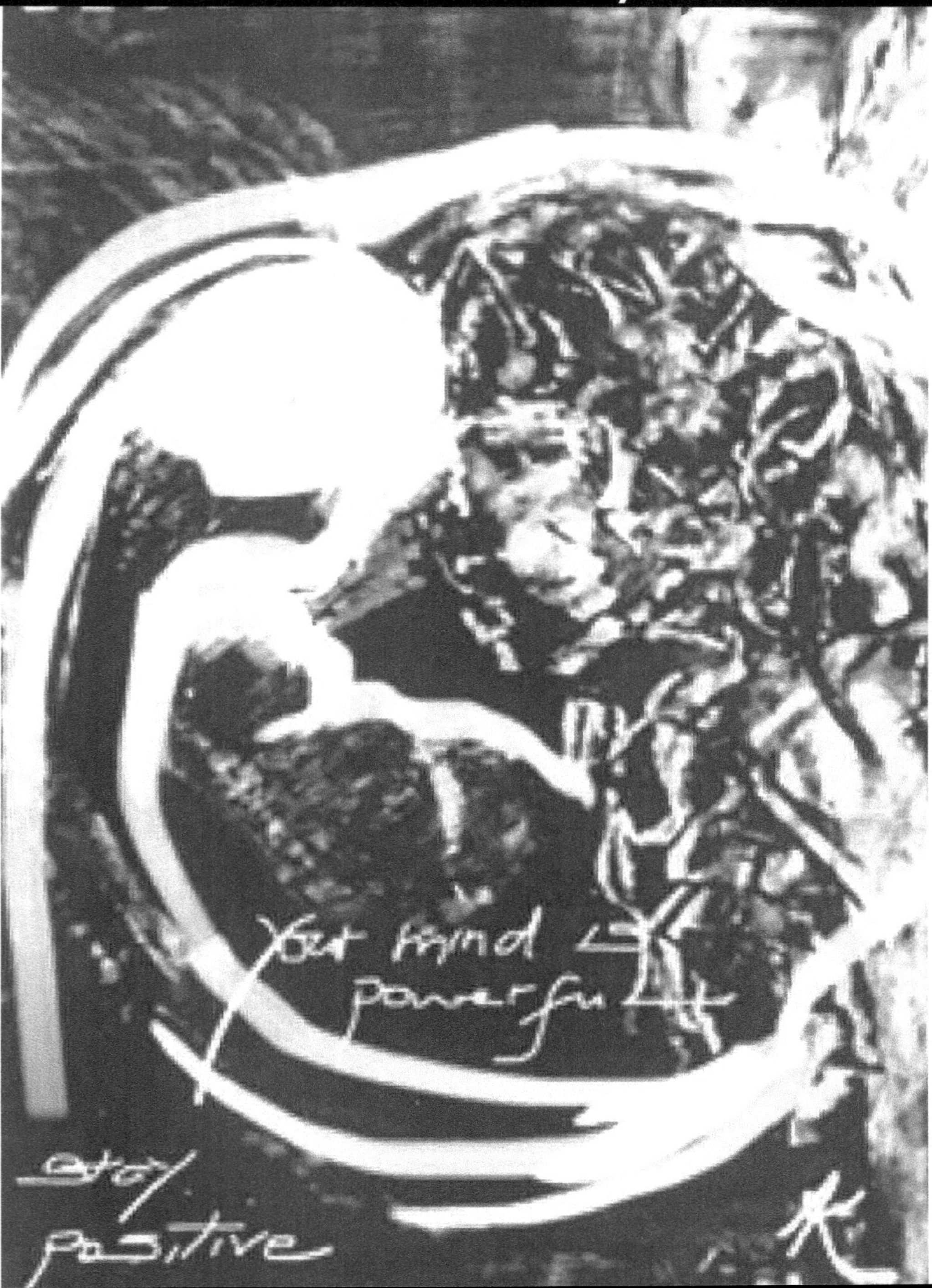

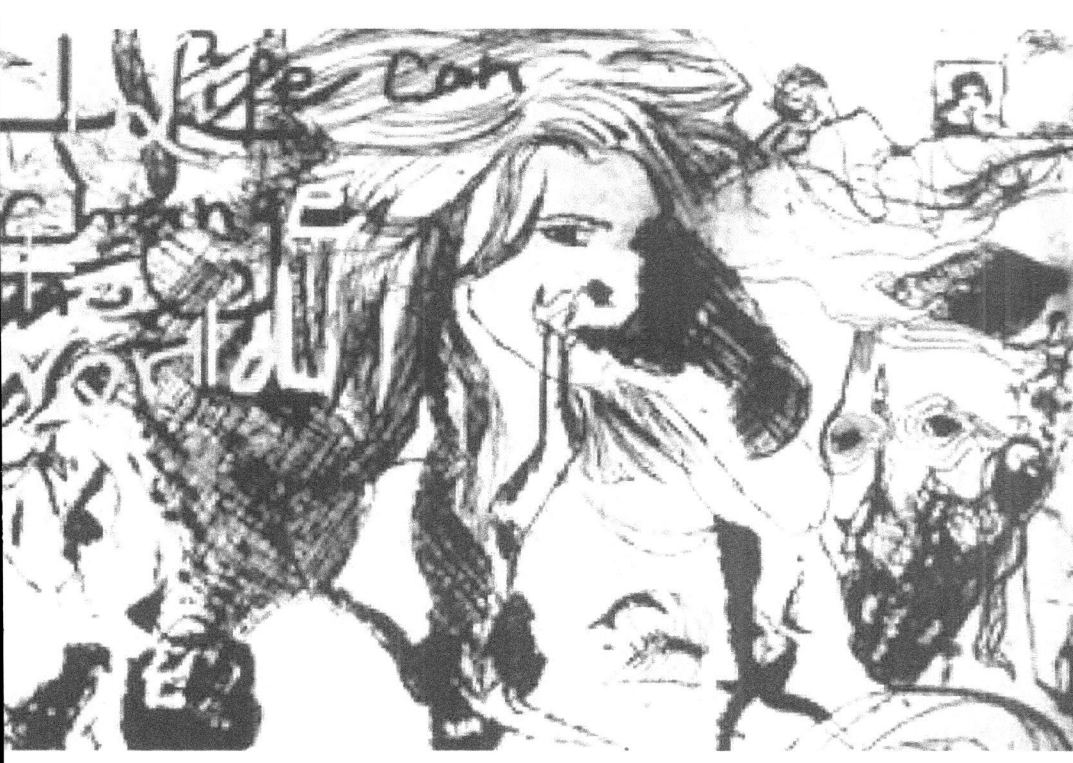

No one can replace You

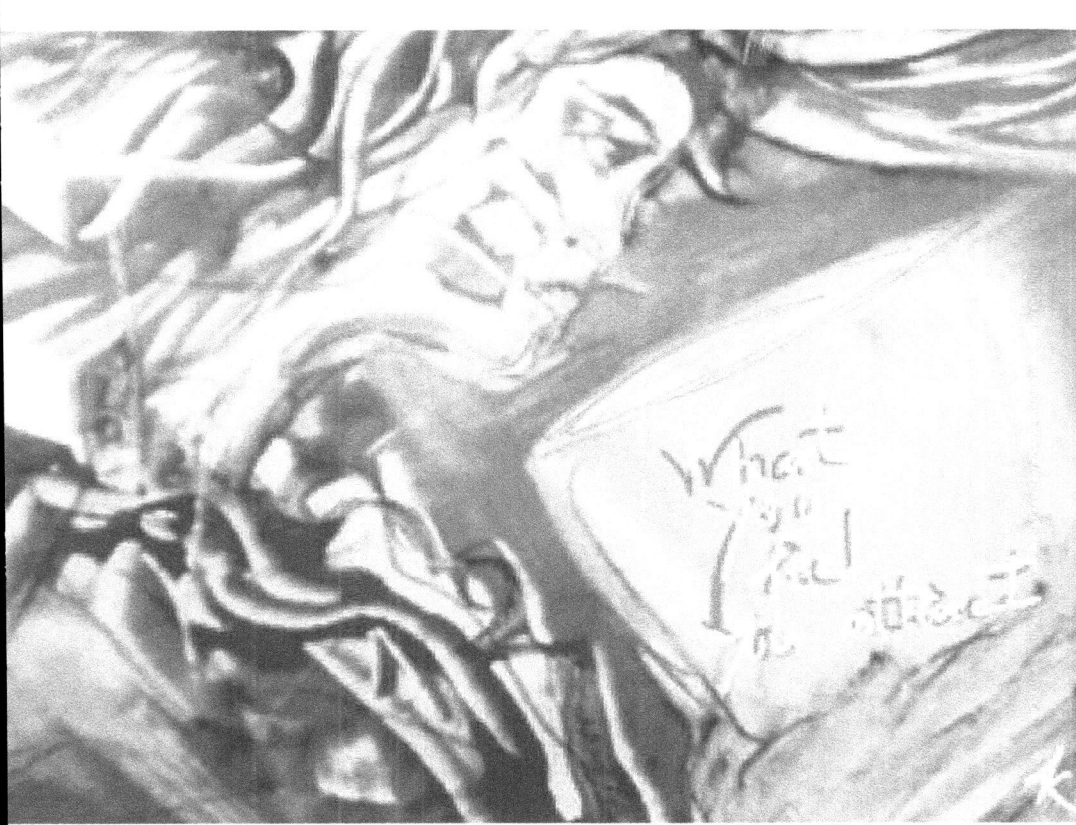

wHere you are going is Here

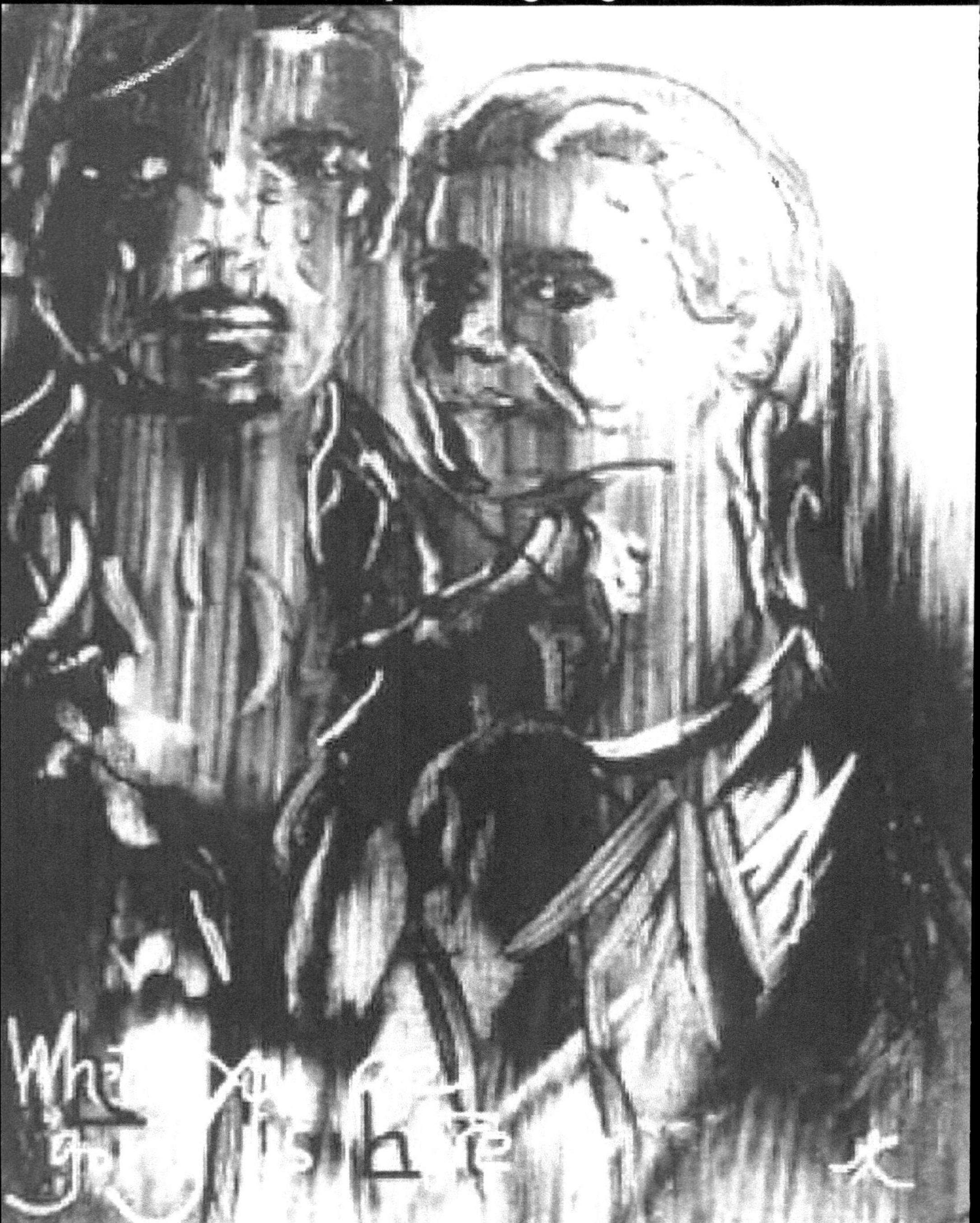

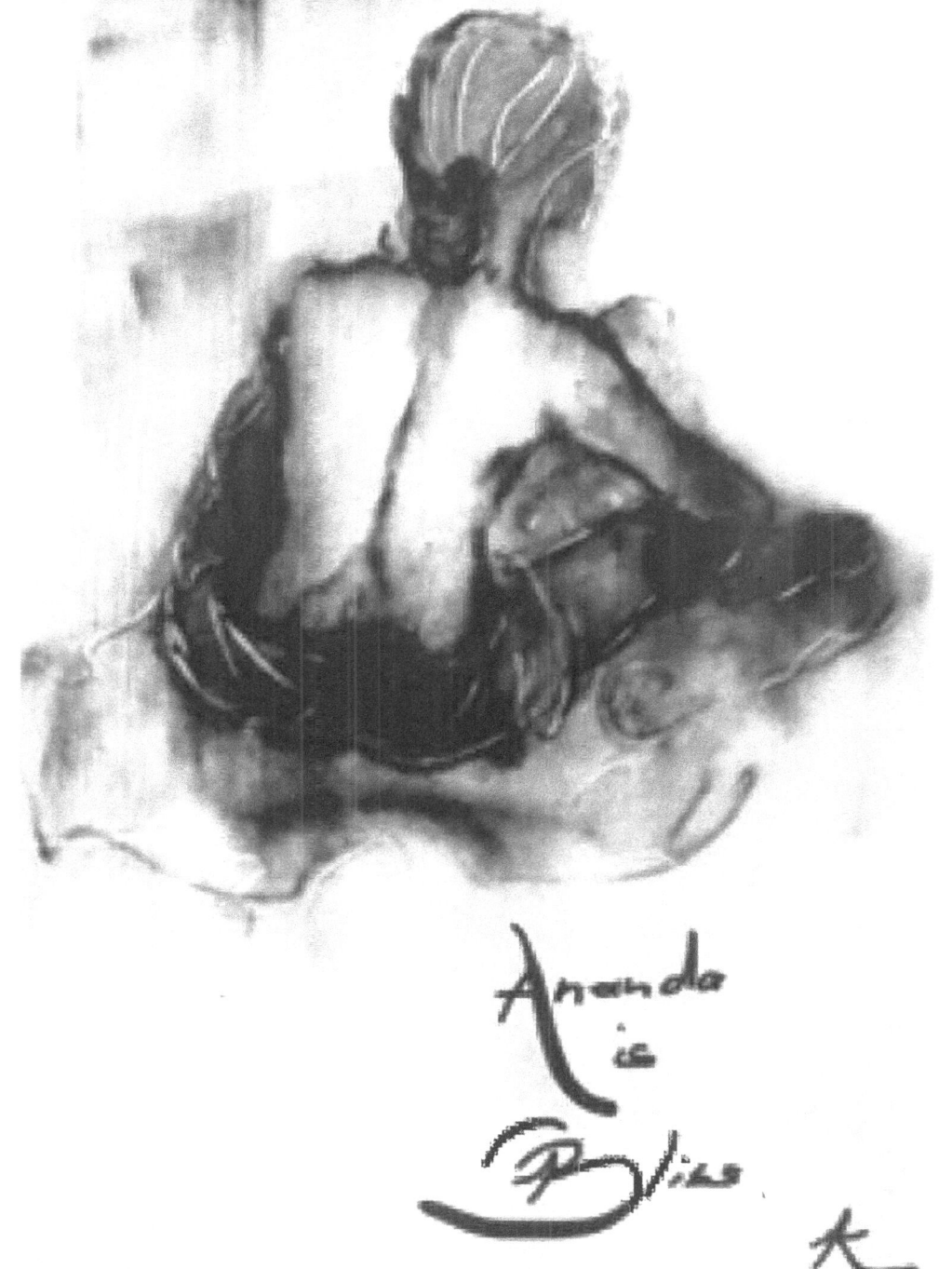

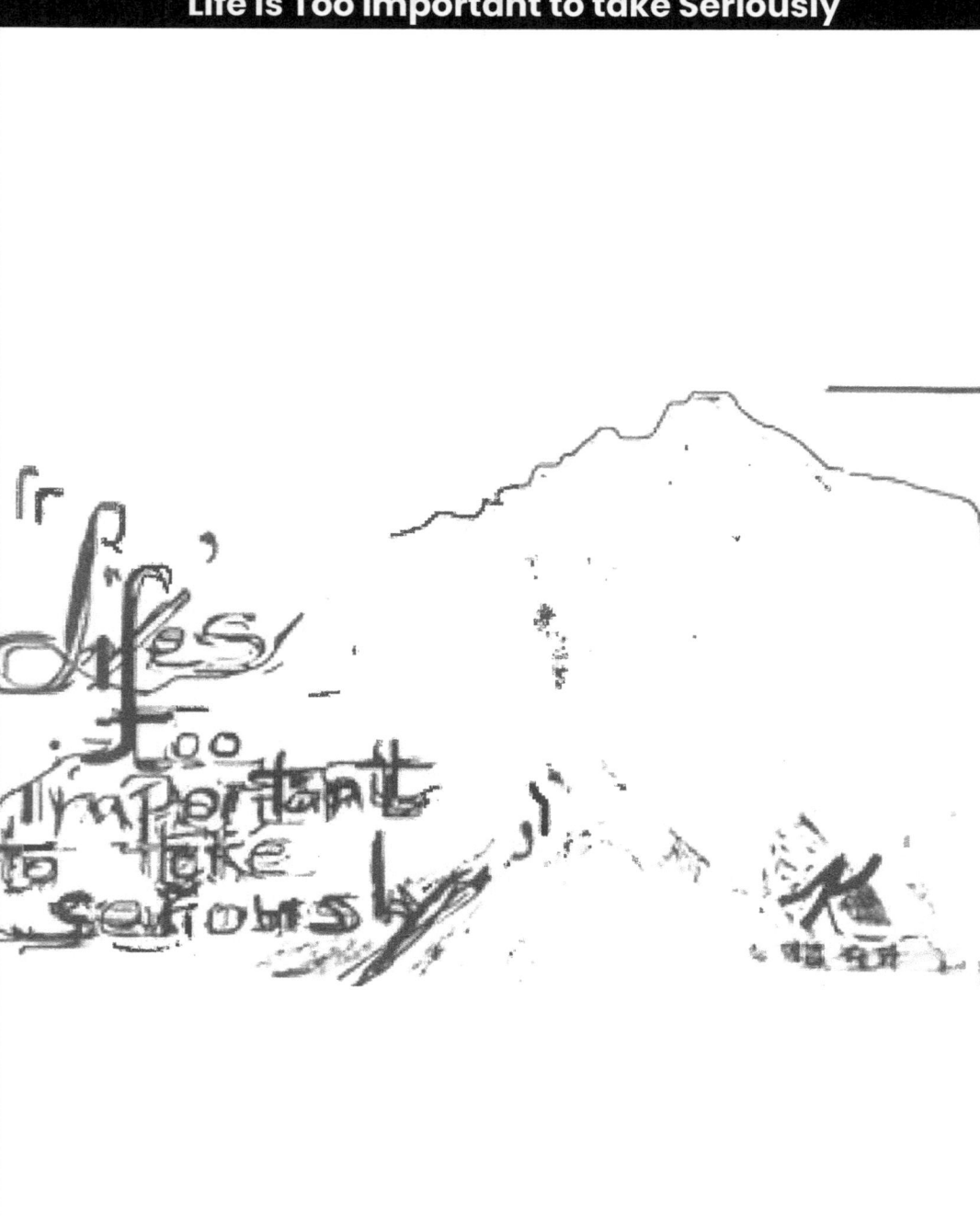

Wherever You Are, Whatever You Do, Be in Love

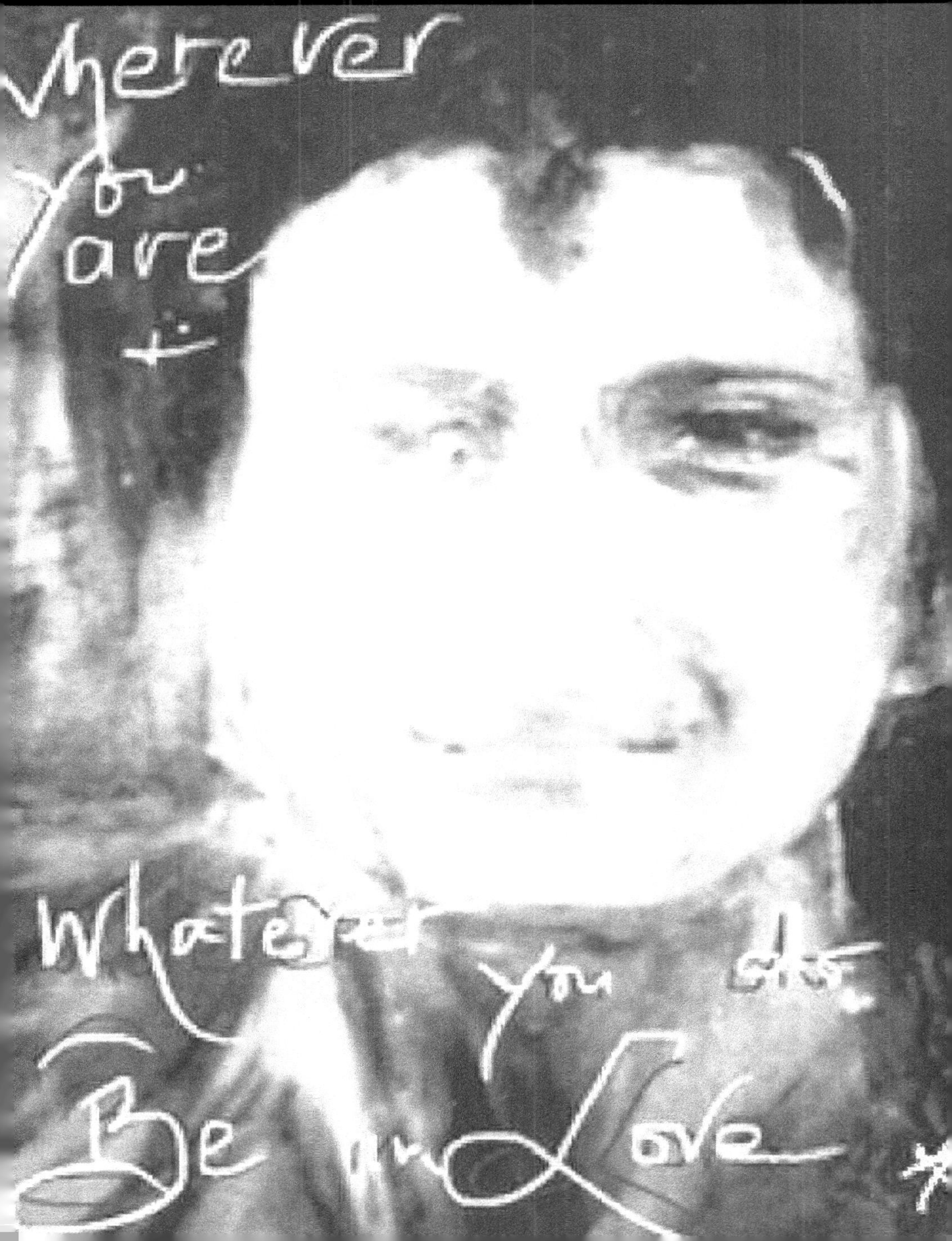

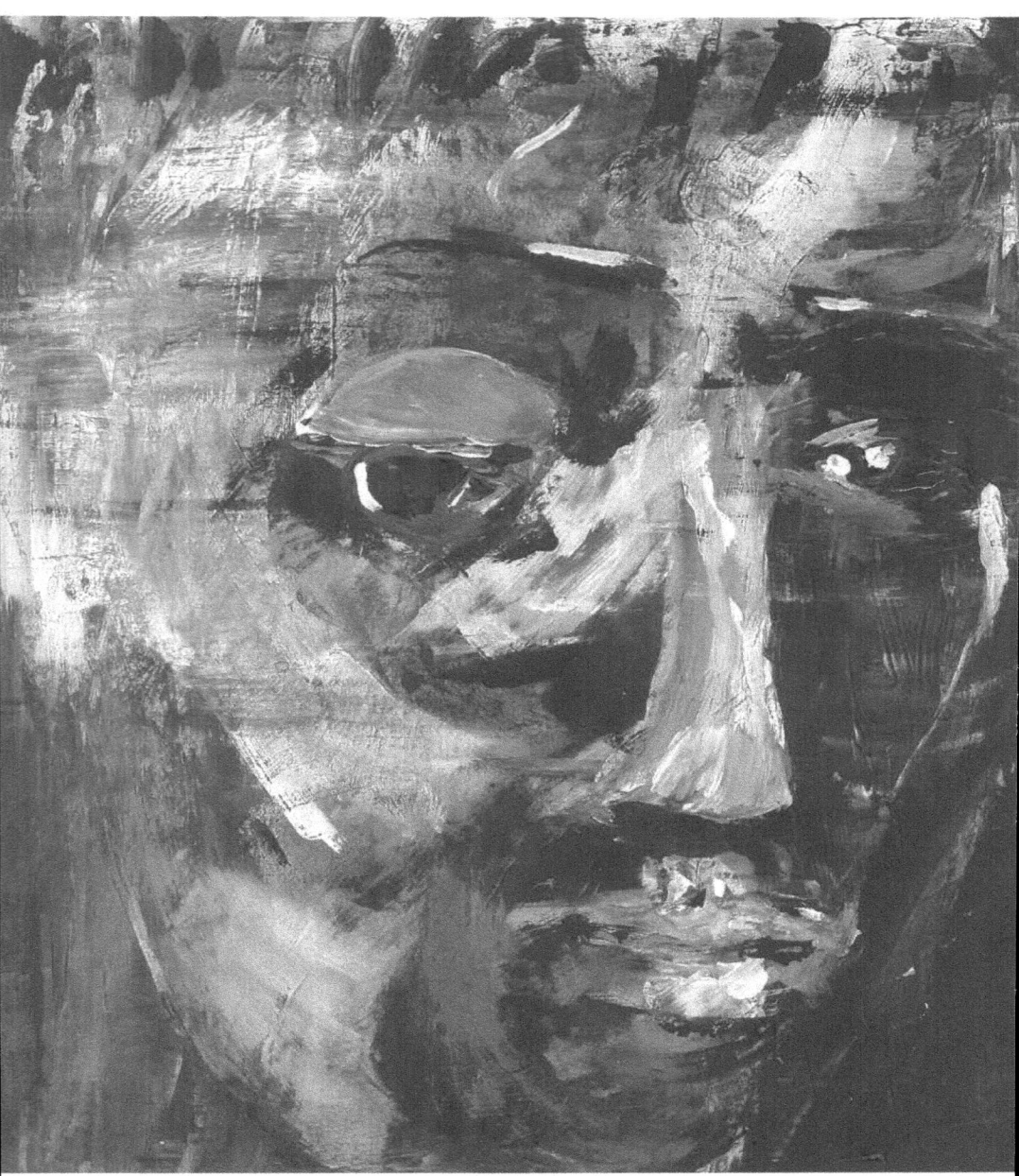

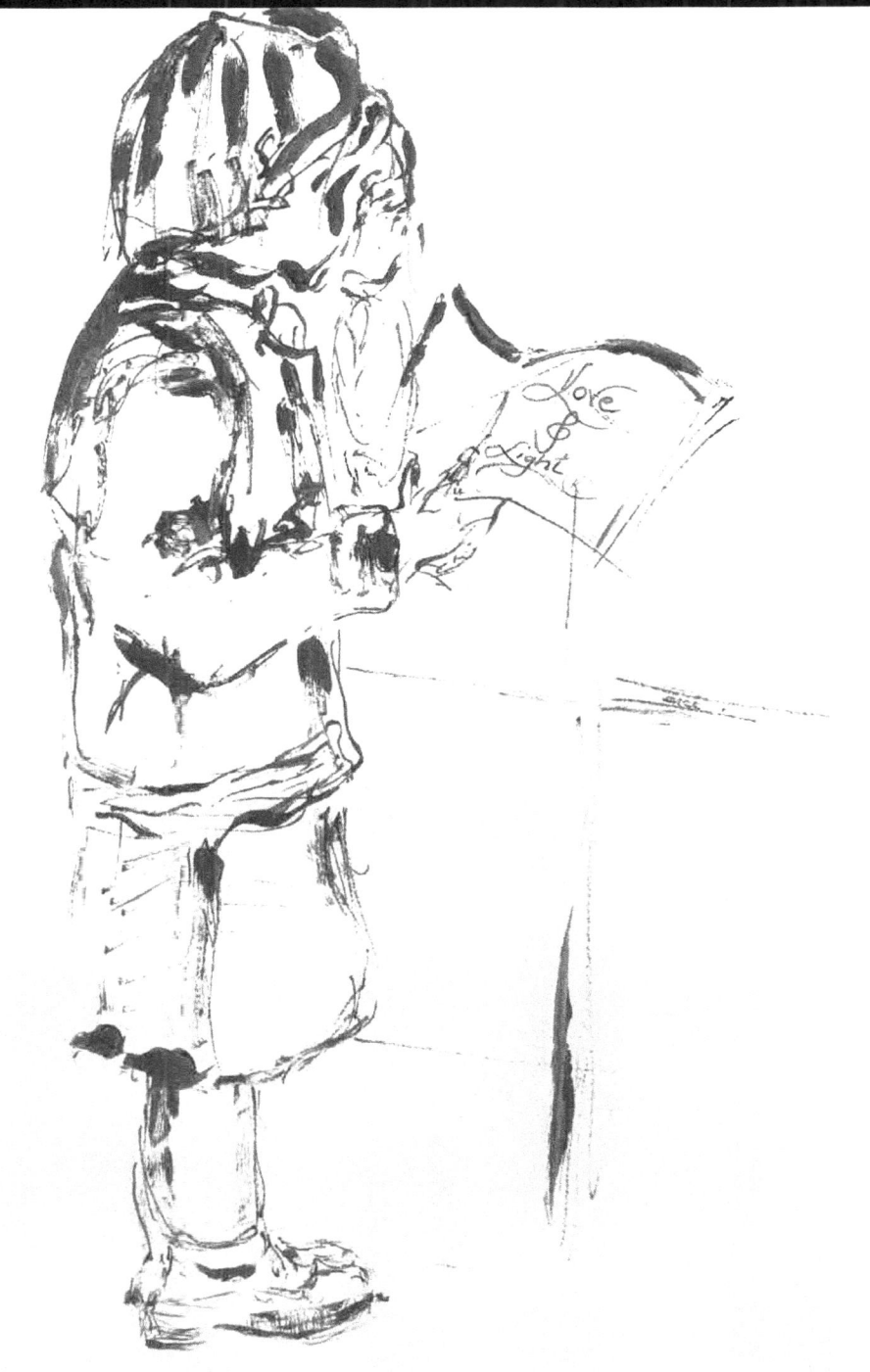

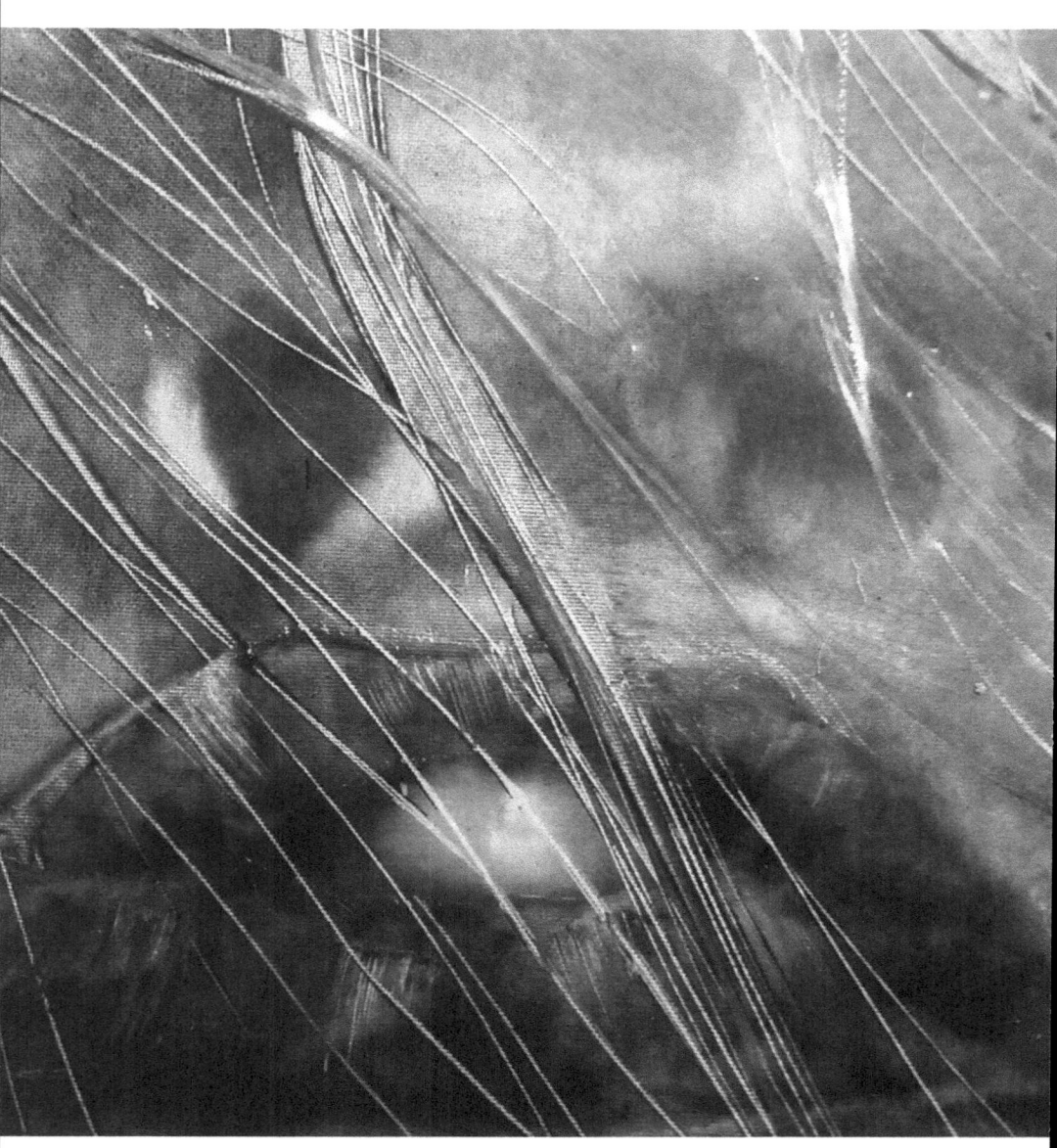

You are a Soul; You have a Body

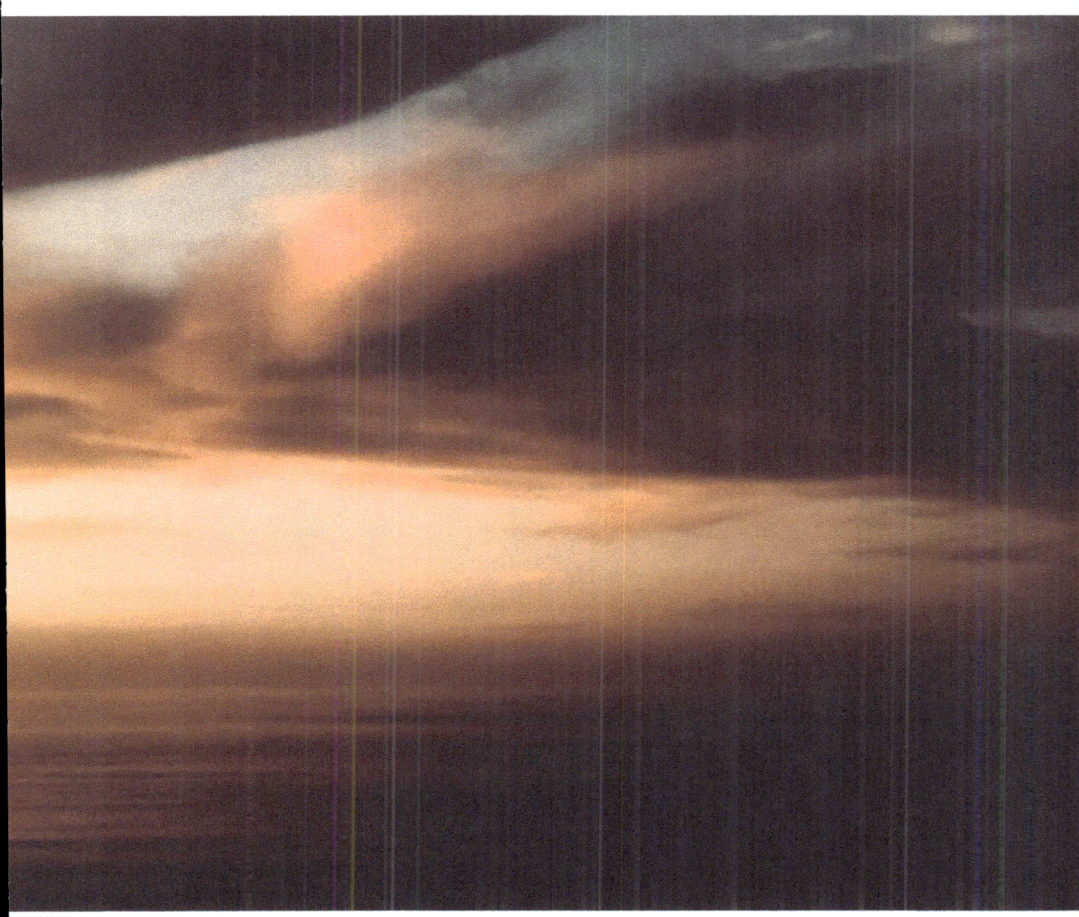

THE END